FIREPOWER OF THE INDIAN INDEPENDENCE STRUGGLE

THE SAGA OF THE REVOLUTION AND THE REVOLUTIONARIES

PRATHAMESH GOVIND MENDKI

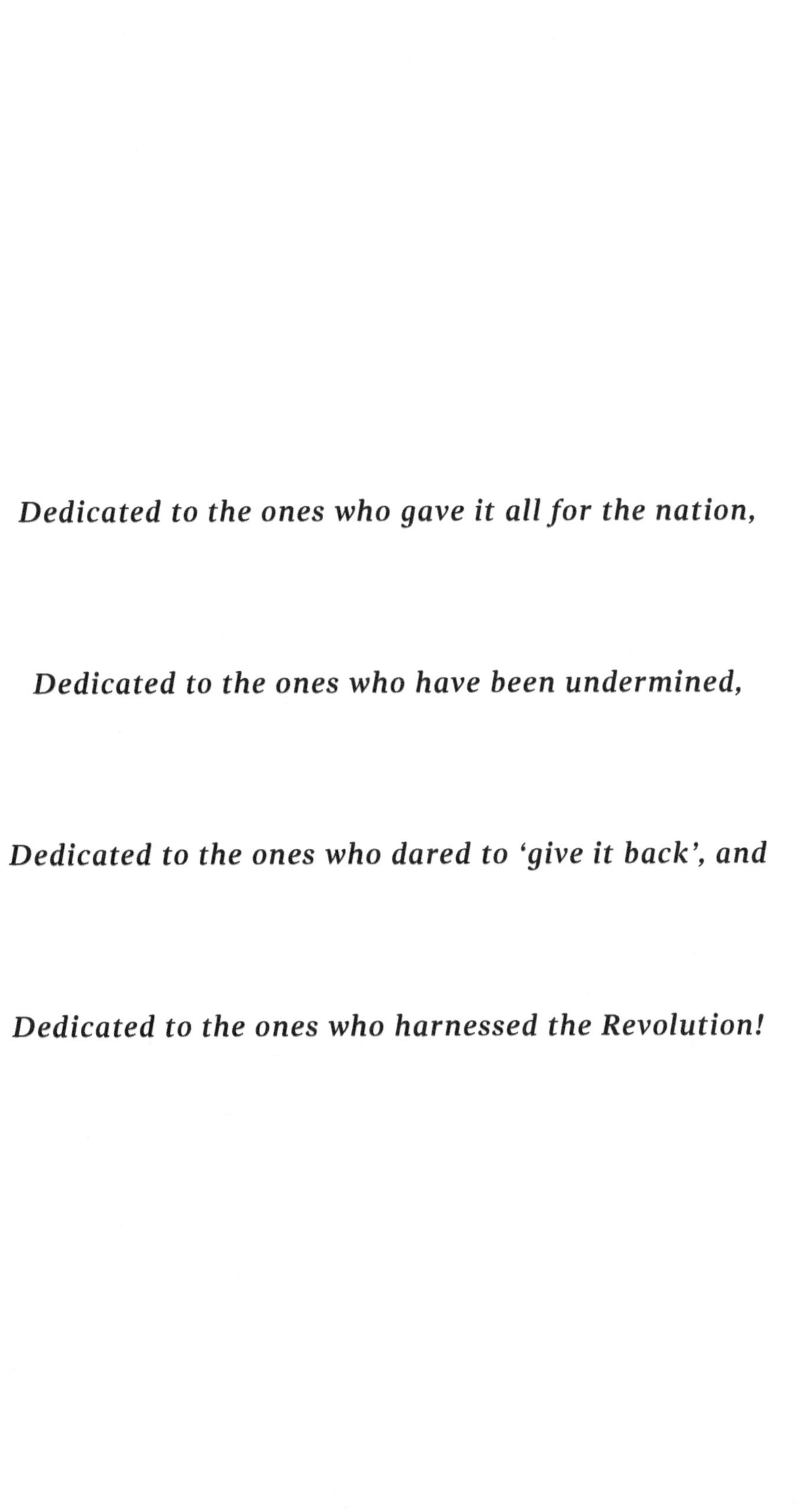

Dedicated to the ones who gave it all for the nation,

Dedicated to the ones who have been undermined,

Dedicated to the ones who dared to 'give it back', and

Dedicated to the ones who harnessed the Revolution!

Contents

Preface   *vii*

  1. VASUDEV BALWANT PHADKE   1

  2. CHAPEKAR BROTHERS   11

  3. ALLURI SITARAMA RAJU   19

  4. KHUDIRAM BOSE   32

  5. SWATANTRAVEER VINAYAK DAMODAR SAVARKAR   46

  6. MADANLAL DHINGRA   62

  7. RAMPRASAD BISMIL AND ASHFAQULLAH KHAN   79

  8. CHANDRASHEKHAR AZAD   100

  9. BHAGAT SINGH, SUKHDEV AND RAJGURU   116

10. SURYA SEN   127

11. PRITILATA WADDEDAR   139

12. SUNITI CHOUDHURY   147

13. SARDAR UDHAM SINGH   153

14. NETAJI SUBHASH CHANDRA BOSE   164

15. CAPTAIN LAXMI SAHGAL   174

An 'Homage'...   181

BIBLIOGRAPHY   183

Preface

India's past is laced with strands of bravery, sacrifice, and a steadfast spirit of resistance. From the earliest civilizations that flourished along the banks of the Indus River to the modern republic that stands tall today, India has always been a land of gallant personalities. These are individuals who have risen against tyranny, injustice, and oppression, often at great personal cost. The essence of this indomitable spirit is captured in the lives and deeds of the revolutionaries who played a pivotal role in India's struggle for independence in the late 19th and 20th centuries. "Firepower of the Indian Independence Struggle" is a tribute to these heroes who embraced the path of armed revolution to free their motherland from colonial rule.

India's heritage is rich with tales of bravery and resilience. From the valorous Rajputs of Mewar who defended their forts and kingdoms against invaders to the Marathas who challenged the might of the Mughal Empire, the narrative of Indian history is replete with examples of fighting back against overwhelming odds. This legacy of gallantry is not confined to the pages of ancient and medieval history. Still, it extends into the modern era, where it found new expression in the fight against British colonialism. The revolutionaries who took up arms against the British were the torchbearers of this legacy. They were driven by a deep sense of patriotism and a burning desire to see their motherland free. They believed that armed resistance was not just a necessity but a moral duty to reclaim the sovereignty that foreign powers had usurped. Their stories are not just accounts of battles and bloodshed but also immense courage, strategic insight, and an unyielding commitment to the cause of freedom.

The 'fighting back' mentality is deeply embedded in India's cultural and historical consciousness. It is a principle that has helped our root civilization stay alive to date. In the face of invasions, internal strife, and foreign domination, the Indian spirit has always found ways to resist and endure. This resilience is not merely about physical combat but encompasses a broader spectrum of resistance, including intellectual, cultural, and spiritual defiance. The Indian independence struggle is an outstanding example of this multifaceted resistance. While the non-violent movement led by Mahatma Gandhi garnered global attention and support, there was also a parallel stream of armed resistance that played a crucial role in weakening the British hold on India. The revolutionaries, through their acts of defiance, inspired millions and created a sense of urgency and momentum that was indispensable to the larger freedom movement.

History is not just a record of past events; it is a repository of collective memory and wisdom that shapes the present and guides the future. Comprehending our history is crucial for several reasons. It helps us appreciate the sacrifices made by our ancestors, understand the roots of our current societal structures, and draw lessons that are relevant to contemporary challenges. For a nation like India, with its diverse and complex past, history serves as a unifying thread that binds its people together. The stories of the revolutionaries are an integral part of this historical narrative. They remind us of a time when ordinary men and women performed extraordinary feats for freedom. These stories are not just about the individuals involved but also about the larger socio-political context in which they operate. They highlight the oppressive policies of the colonial regime, the economic exploitation, and the cultural suppression that ignited the spark of rebellion in the hearts of many.

Storytelling is a powerful medium that can bring history to life. It can engage, inspire, and educate in ways that mere factual recounting cannot. Through storytelling, we can connect with the emotions, motivations, and experiences of historical figures, making their lives and struggles more relatable and impactful. In writing "Firepower of the Indian Independence Struggle", the aim is not just to chronicle the events and exploits of the revolutionaries but to delve deeper into their psyche, their motivations, and their dreams. By weaving their stories into a cohesive narrative, this book seeks to create a vivid and compelling portrait of the armed resistance movement. It is an attempt to honour the memory of these heroes and ensure that their contributions are remembered and celebrated by future generations.

The question of 'why' this book was written is as important as the stories it contains. The revolutionaries of India's independence struggle have often been overshadowed by the more prominent narrative of non-violent resistance. While the significance of non-violence cannot be understated, it is equally important to recognize and honour the contributions of those who chose a different path. Their stories are a testament to the diversity of thought and approach that characterized the freedom movement. Also, there's this 'unquenched thirst' of providing justice to your great ancestor who, despite giving their whole lives for the nation, had been wronged, vilified, undermined and unjustly portrayed by a particular diaspora over the years. Storytelling, hence, is a great way to debunk that portrayal and throw a light upon the black, white and grey matter of the prominent historical figures. There is also a pressing need to bridge the gap between the past and the present. In an era where historical narratives are often simplified or distorted, it is crucial to present a balanced and nuanced account of our struggle for independence. By focusing on the revolutionaries, this book aims to provide a more comprehensive understanding of the movement and highlight the multiplicity of efforts that culminated in India's freedom.

Moreover, this book is a response to the growing interest in India's revolutionary past among young Indians. As the inheritors of a rich and complex legacy, they need to know and appreciate the sacrifices made by their forebears. By bringing these stories to light, the book seeks to inspire a sense of pride, responsibility, and a deeper connection to our shared heritage. From Vasudev Balwant Phadke, who is often regarded as the father of the armed struggle against British rule, to Captain Laxmi Sehgal, who led the Rani of Jhansi Regiment of the Indian National Army, the book covers a wide spectrum of revolutionary figures. Each of these personalities brought their unique strengths and perspectives to the movement, enriching it in the process.

Phadke's guerrilla tactics, the bravery of the Chapekar brothers, the strategic brilliance of Bhagat Singh, the resilience of Subhas Chandra Bose, the sheer determination of Swatantraveer Vinayak Damodar Savarkar and the leadership of Captain Sehgal are just a few examples of the diverse approaches to armed resistance. Their stories are intertwined with the broader narrative of India's quest for freedom, providing a holistic view of the movement.

"Firepower of the Indian Independence Struggle"is more than just a historical account; it is a tribute to the indomitable spirit of India's revolutionaries. It seeks to illuminate the path they paved, the challenges they faced, and the legacy they left behind. By exploring their lives and contributions, the book aims to foster a deeper understanding of the armed struggle and its significance in the broader context of India's independence movement. In celebrating these gallant personalities, we not only honour their memory but also draw inspiration for the present and future. Their stories remind us of the power of courage, determination, and the will to fight for what is right. As we navigate the complexities of the modern world, these timeless values continue to hold relevance, guiding us towards a just and equitable society.

In the end, I'd like to just say that I have tried my best to present the history as it is through the method of storytelling. This book, by no means, is a part of any political agenda and nor does it aim to set a particular narrative against anything or anyone. This is the least I can do for the great personalities we've had in the past, and I really hope that through this book, may their stories resonate with readers, inspiring a renewed sense of pride in our heritage and a commitment to uphold the principles for which they fought and sacrificed.

Vande Mataram!

CHAPTER ONE

VASUDEV BALWANT PHADKE

Revolutionary - A person who not only aspires and thrives hard to bring out a blazing revolution, but also aims to change the face of society to the core, at large. A person who becomes a source of inspiration for future generations of other revolutionaries and different revolutionary groups, which constantly strive to seize the independence that they deserve from the imperialistic forces and take their country out of the imbroglio state of affairs of the tyrants. India is no exception, as she has produced a plethora of names who have worked their fingers to the bone to tremble the cruel, unjust and oppressive foreign forces.

In the times of spectacular names in the world of revolution, such as Giuseppe Mazzini, Giuseppe Garibaldi and Otto Von Bismarck, was born an Indian Krantikari who not only gave the British nightmares but also became the rightful source of inspiration for the upcoming generations. Today known as the "Father of the Modern Indian Revolutionary Movement", Vasudev Balwant Phadke is unfortunately a lesser-known name still today amongst the Indian diaspora. A stern, sturdy and no-nonsense man from Pune, he revived the hope that was systematically suppressed and subverted by the Brits after the revolution of 1857.

Vasudev Balwant Phadke was one of the early contemporary Indian revolutionaries who took up arms to drive out the British. This restless energy ignited a flame that grew into a powerful firestorm of the Indian liberation fight, in which many Indians fought and perished until India gained its independence. His unwavering bravery, idealistic aspirations, and selflessness contributed to the country's awakening and accelerated the rise of political consciousness. He ought to have a special place among the national leaders and freedom warriors because of his fitness for things. He was an idol for countless martyrs who came after him, and his life was an epic of labour, sweat, blood, and tears. Vasudev Phadke publicly declared our desire for complete political independence, even when educated gurus and notable politicians hesitated. He was the first Indian leader to urge the populace to fight against foreign authority and to spread the slogan 'Swaraj' from village to village.

Vasudev Balwant Phadke - The Father of the Indian Armed Revolution.

Early Life and Formative Years

The Phadkes were Brahmins from Chitpavan who belonged to the same caste as Pune's illustrious Peshwas. The family was from the Konkan village of Kelshi, which is located in the Ratnagiri area. It moved to the Kolaba district's Shirdhon in the 16th century. Anantrao, the grandfather of Vasudev Phadke, was in charge of the Karnala fort, which was overlooking Shirdhon, at the time of Peshwa's final defeat in 1818. He did not give up the fort easily. The name 'Subahdar' remained even after the military command was lost in 1818. 'Subahdar' was the moniker given to Vasudev Balwantrao's father and grandfather in their respective communities.

On November 4th, 1845, Balvantrao and his wife Saraswatibai welcomed a son, and they named him Vasudev. He was naturally rebellious since he was young and despite this nature, his grandparents, with whom he was raised, gave him a lot of care. He enjoyed living outdoors, trained in riding, wrestling, and fencing, and eventually became an accomplished marksman. However, he had little interest in reading books. When Vasudev's grandfather Anantrao died, he was 10 years old. Vasudev's way of life also came to an end when his father started paying particular attention to his son's attendance at school. He attended a primary school in Kalyan for 4 years before moving to Bombay and Pune to study English.

Vasudev Balwant wed Saibai in 1859. After a brief illness, she passed away in 1872, leaving her only daughter Mathutai. In 1873, he remarried Gopikabai, who dispelled from her mind any thoughts of personal need or ornamentation. Her altruism won her husband's respect. Vasudev Balwant valued his wife's virtues greatly. While it was not widely accepted at the time, he held progressive ideas on women's education. He sometimes taught Gopikabai classes with his brothers, since he had a strong desire for her to receive an education. As a result, Gopikabai was able to memorise Sanskrit texts and recite the "Amarkosh" with ease. Vasudev, a skilled fighter with a sword, also taught his wife how to ride a horse and shoot an arrow.

Following Vasudev's graduation, his family held three large-scale festivities: his brother's thread ceremony and the marriage ceremonies of two of his sisters. These events significantly strained the Phadke family's finances. Vasudev therefore started working as a clerk for the Great Indian Peninsular Railway in Bombay not long after his first marriage. He then accepted a position at the Grant Medical College, one of India's oldest medical schools. He accepted a new position in the Military Finance Department in 1864, and in 1865, he was moved to the department's Poona office.

Phadke's temperament made him unfit to hold a subordinate role. Vasudev's youthful resentment of his employers was fueled by the demanding nature of his work, the soulless discipline of the office, and the dominance of his foreign superiors. Vasudev Balwant Phadke turned to spirituality for holistic comfort briefly. He was taught academic knowledge of ancient texts and pious practices such as Sandhya, Purushasukta, Rudra & Payamana under the guidance of an educated priest named Vinayakbhat

Varze. He also continued to be deeply absorbed in the worship of his principal deity, Dattatraya. He also travelled a lot to see numerous saints in an attempt to find the ultimate truth.

But during the course of such events, especially in the 1860s, Vasudev had begun to despise the British to its core. Their lifestyle, their attitude towards the 'non-whites', their discriminatory nature against even the most loyal 'native' workforce and their noticeable atrocities against the poor Indian diaspora, were forging Vasudev's conscience against the British. Subconsciously, a substantial groundwork was being laid for all those gallant tremors that Vasudev was about to give to the British Empire in the subsequent years to come. A significant occasion in 1870 turned out to be a turning point in Vasudev Phadke's life. Due to a delay in obtaining leave from his workplace, Vasudev was unable to be present at his mother's bedside as she passed away. He reprimanded the authorities in the greatest terms, his frustration and wrath knowing no bounds. A year later, he was denied permission to carry out his mother's death anniversary rites once more. This made him even more resentful of the British rule and strengthened his determination to work towards India's political independence.

The Tragedy, The Distress and A 'Revolutionary' Metamorphosis...

Now, the evolving political landscape in the Deccan in the 1870s provided both validation and impetus for Vasudev's determination to launch an uprising against the British Raj. The Poona Sarvajanik Sabha (People's Organisation of Pune) established the nation's first political front for public agitation in Poona in 1870. Under the principal direction of Mahadev Govind Ranade, it operated in full swing and aimed at empowering the masses to transform them into well-educated and patriotic Bharatiya. In December 1872, Ranade gave his first lecture on "National Trade" in Poona. Using statistical facts and analysis, he exposed the harm done to India's economy as a result of its careless and uncontrolled use of imported commodities. Many young people were drawn to his erudite speech, including Vasudev Balwant Phadke.

Vasudev's public life began at the same time as Ranade's lectures, which fueled his inner flame of patriotism. Both of them (Ranade and Phadke) hated India's exploitation under foreign authority as contemporaries.

However, their political ideologies were distinguishable. Vasudev's instant armed uprising was the response to the national ills, while Ranade's was limited to prayers and pleas to the British Government. It's a noteworthy fact that Vasudev Balwant Phadke was the prophet of revolutionary ideology, while Ranade was the founder of constitutionalism. They stood for two different political schools of thought that Indians adopted during their generations till the nation gained its independence.

The Deccan peasantry experienced increasing suffering during the years 1870-1878. The peasantry was being asked to pay 50% to 100% more than before due to stricter tax collecting practises and revision-time assessment increases. The Deccan district had a prolonged drought, despite a sharp increase in the demand for revenue. Barren pastures and withering plants provided little food for animals or people. The Deccan turned into an actual dust bowl. A sharp shortage of food grains caused prices to skyrocket. The government's efforts to alleviate the famine were ineffective in easing suffering. The end effect was a shortage of food and an epidemic-like cholera and fever outbreak. 8 lakh people were estimated to have died in the famine by the Famine Commission in 1880. Farmers were forced to become landless workers or little more than tenants working in their own fields as a result of government laws and regulations that favoured moneylenders in the payment of taxes and settlement of agricultural debts. Tight forest regulations and a decrease in grazing areas exacerbated the misery of the lowest castes in the villages and among the tribal people, adding to the overall environment of hopelessness and despair.

The increasing distress impacted Vasudev deeply. According to him, foreign rule was to blame for the devastation of Indian industry, disregard for irrigation, and scarcity of food and clothing for the average person. In his autobiography, he described how he felt this way: "Thinking day and night of these and a thousand other sorrows, my mind was concentrated upon the overthrow of the British dominion in India. I had nothing else on my mind. The thought tormented me. I used to wake up in the middle of the night and think about how the British would fail, practically driving me insane". Phadke began giving speeches in public on the terrible situation facing the nation. He vigorously criticised the authorities while touring the Deccan districts. He echoed the American philosopher Henry David Thoreau when he declared that everyone had the right to oppose and reject the government when its oppression or incompetence was extreme and intolerable. He urged his compatriots to work towards independence, saying that Swaraj was the only solution to their problems.

But, the divine proposal seemed absurd to the educated class, to whom Phadke urged to rise up in rebellion against the British. To plan a rebellion, he resorted to the Ramoshis, Kolis, Bhils, and Dhangars. These people, who had been severely impacted by the ongoing drought, listened obediently to the call of someone they held in high regard as their saviour. He assembled a group of roughly 300 fervent men around him and proceeded to work towards his goal of destroying the British authority in India. Vasudev Balwant Phadke now devised a plan to send his men to various regions of the nation to obstruct government operations and foster chaos. He believed that nationwide panic would result from outbreaks occurring at the same time in every region. The movement of news across the nation would be completely halted as a result of the stopping of oaks, railway lines, and telegraph cables. He anticipated that thousands would join him in this chaotic situation, accomplishing his goal of creating an Indian Republic.

The Tempest Unleashed and a Furious Onslaught...!

Arms and money were what Phadke needed to realise his magnificent design. He started negotiating with the wealthy to get them to contribute the money needed for the insurrection. Phadke assured them that the funds were needed to achieve Swaraj and would be returned once the objective was met. Phadke paused to reflect when the wealthy's attitude defied his expectations: "Means do not by themselves matter. Why not take away the wealthy men's riches by force to add to the cash for Swaraj if they are unwilling to provide it voluntarily?" Vasudev was a well-read man and he knew what Chhatrapati Shivaji Maharaj had to do with the wealthy self-declared aristocrats (who were businessmen and traders by profession) when he sacked Surat twice. Purity was running in the veins of his conscience and he was willing to do the same if our 'own' weren't ready to contribute.

Intending to fortify the muscles of war, the men raised by Phadke from the affluent strata in the countryside started a systematic campaign of plundering and dacoity. The first raid happened on the evening of February 23, 1879, when Phadke, with a sizable party, broke into the Pune district village of Dhamari. The haughty Marwaris had their estates burned and their homes ransacked. After leaving Dhamari, the group proceeded to Davi Nimbgaon, Jejuri, and Panmala. Following the 5th March battle on Valhe, the rebels moved into Bhor territory and began robbing the wealthy residents of Chandkhed, Savargoan, Harnai, and Mangdari. The ones who donated the money wholeheartedly were not at all harmed and earned the great goodwill of Phadke's men, who held them in very high regard as they had also contributed to the noble cause of freeing India from the shackles of the tyrant whites.

It's a noteworthy thing, that Phadke had a very worthwhile endeavour for fighting his war. He had instructed his men under tight instructions not to harm children, aged people and/or harass women during raids. As word of Vasudev Balwant Phadke's uprising appeared in newspapers, the political climate in the nation became electrified, and people throughout India found it difficult to understand the true ramifications of the Deccan uprising. By now, the government was aware of the threat and had assembled specialised equipment to locate the rebels. Relentlessly, in May 1879, Phadke declared that the Government would face severe repercussions if it did not supply inexpensive food grains, give jobs to the ryots (the common people), lower general taxation, and cut the pay of its European commanders. By offering a counteroffer for the governor's and other officials' heads, the government mocked its offer of a reward for his capture.

The well-known 'Vasudev Proclamation' was a statement that publicly condemned the British policy of exploiting India economically and demanded that the ryots receive financial assistance as a matter of inherent justice. During the Indian independence movement, it was the first audacious challenge of its sort to the British Government. Now, the government moved quickly to apprehend the rebel commander, Vasudev Balwant Phadke. Major Henry William Daniell, the District Superintendent of Police, was tasked with finding and apprehending Phadke after learning of his identity as the rebel commander. He was also acquainted with the province's challenging area.

Meanwhile, Phadke found out he had been duped by the Ramoshis, who comprised the majority of his following. The loot they took was all that worried them, and their leader's extravagant plan did not pique their curiosity. Phadke looked south after becoming disillusioned with the Ramoshis. He went to Nizam's domain and attempted to rally the Arabs and Rohillas to his cause. Throughout the province, Major Daniell increased security measures and issued precautionary instructions. But the actions were ineffective. Vasudev's name resonated across the nation, and his noble dread eventually spread throughout Maharashtra. He became a household legend among the 'Maratha' people.

Phadke was being followed by the police, who learned of his whereabouts in the south. On July 17, 1879, Major Daniell arrived in Hyderabad in the evening. He made a direct drive to the British Residency, where he met with Sir Richard Meade, who informed the Nizam of Daniell's arrival. The Nizam, the British Government's most devoted supporter, quickly joined the search for Vasudev Balwant Phadke. A few of the Rohillas turned traitor and revealed Vasudev's precise position, terrified of the wrath of their Huzurs. On the night of July 20, 1879, he was finally apprehended in the Bijapur district near Devar Navadgi. Just like Panipat (1761), the gullible Rohillas proved their treacherous 'loyalty' towards the outsiders for their own filthy gains and thus, 'the turbulence was now being eased' by the British.

The Transportation for Life, and the Legacy...

Vasudev Balwant Phadke and 14 of his associates were tried in Pune on November 3, 1879, on allegations of dacoity and conspiracy with dacoits to wage war against the Queen, gather troops and weapons for the war, and incite discontent against the government. The two main pieces of evidence presented against him were his journal and the autobiography he had written while staying at the Srisaila Mallikarjuna a few months prior.

It was with great courage that Ganesh Vasudev Joshi, also referred to as Kaka Joshi, stood up on his own to defend Phadke in court. In his declaration before the Court, Phadke stated categorically, *"It is due to the British rule that India had become a prey to starvation deaths. Our industries are being destroyed. The goods from England are exempted from taxes so that we cannot run any industry in our country ... I could only think of one method to save these people from total destruction, i.e., the liberation from the British yoke. Day and night there is but one prayer in my heart; but one thought in my mind. Oh God, even if my life is lost, let my country be free, let my countrymen be happy. I have taken up arms, raised an army and rebelled against the British Government with this single aim. Today, this is the duty of every Indian. I could not succeed. But someday someone will succeed. Oh my countrymen, forgive me for my failure"*.

However, his own journal, memoirs, and confessions, along with the testimony of several witnesses gathered by the prosecution, provided ample evidence for all the charges. Upon being found guilty of the accusations the jury had brought against him, Mr Newnham, the judge, condemned him to life in prison, which at the time was a more agonising punishment than death. The path to deport Phadke to the Andaman Islands was now clear following the High Court's denial of the appeal against the sentence. However, the Andaman Islands housed a sizable number of prisoners of war from 1857, with the terms permitting their eventual release from the islands after a predetermined amount of time. The government feared that Phadke, using the facilities, would cause problems in the Andamans with the help of the prisoners. Thus, the Andaman was substituted for the less expansive, more heavily fortified fort of Aden (Yemen), which housed fewer captives and was directly under the control of the Bombay Presidency, as the destination for his transfer.

Vasudev Balwant Phadke's spirit remained unwavering and strong despite his many hardships while incarcerated. After roughly six months, he started working on his jailbreak strategy. Phadke put the finishing touches on his escape scheme at the beginning of October 1880. After being imprisoned for months, he began his plan on October 12, 1880, and shortly after, he passed the barrier gate and felt the wind of freedom. But his freedom did not last long. While travelling through a foreign nation, he was shortly pursued and taken prisoner by the authorities, again. Vasudev endured severe hardships for the following two and half years. It was not long after the horrendous abuse of excessive workloads and prolonged isolation that he developed tuberculosis in the middle of 1881. Even though he was in such good health, he went on a death fast and insisted on having his fetters taken off and his living arrangements improved. On February 17, 1883, Phadke's condition deteriorated. The doctors gave up hope for his recovery early on that awful day. India's first revolutionary entered the gates of heaven, in the fort of Aden around 4:20 p.m.

For at least three generations, Indian revolutionaries and nationalists found constant inspiration in Vasudev Balwant Phadke, who perpetuated the country's battle. He was a national hero to practically all politically conscious minds and great leaders belonging to diverse schools of political thought, from the late Dr M.R. Jayakar, one of the greatest liberals and constitutionalists, to Swatantryaveer Vinayak Damodar Savarkar, since he was the first rebel against British rule before Tilak entered the arena. The name Vasudev Balwant Phadke will shine brighter than ever in the annals of the Indian liberation movement, as long as the terms of Indian nationalism and national gratitude for the land's sacrifices endure!

CHAPTER TWO

CHAPEKAR BROTHERS

To begin with, there are countless anecdotes and real-life stories of how the Britishers tortured and tormented the Indians whenever they got even a petty reason to do it! But as a matter of pride, many Bravehearts repeatedly roared to resist the oppressive British empire through their daunting and gallant acts of armed revolution. The 22nd of June marks the anniversary of the assassination of the British ICS (Indian Civil Services) officer, Walter Rand who was directly responsible for the horrendous torture and harassment of commoners of Pune. He, along with his assistant Lt. Ayerest was brought to justice on this very day in 1897 which also happened to be the day on which the diamond jubilee of Queen Victoria was being celebrated all over the world, including India!

Numerous men and women gave their lives to free India from the oppressive and unfair British rule that turned the country, which had a GDP of more than 20 in the 1600s, into a poor country by the end of the 19th century. This struggle took place during the early colonial rule under the East India Company and later under the Raj after 1857. The brave freedom fighters who sacrificed their lives so that future generations could breathe clean air and experience complete freedom without any restrictions are gratefully remembered by the entire country. Numerous unsung heroes who are unknown throughout India's length and breadth are among them. These unsung heroes include the Chapekar brothers, who hailed from Maharashtra.

The Chapekar Brothers were Vasudeo Hari Chapekar (1880 - 8 May 1899), also known as Vasudeva or Wasudev, Damodar Hari Chapekar (25 June 1869 - 18 April 1898), and Balkrishna Hari Chapekar (1873 - 12 May 1899, also known as Bapurao) and, in the late 19th century, after the people of Pune had grown upset with the vandalism committed by the officers and soldiers he had hired, they were engaged in the murder of W. C. Rand, the British Plague Commissioner of Pune. Mahadev Vinayak Ranade participated in the murder as well.

The brothers were originally from 'Chapa', a tiny village near Pune, India, called Chinchwad. An Indian Civil Services official named Walter Charles Rand served as the Special Plague Committee's commissioner when the bubonic plague struck India in 1896-1897. To deal with the emergency, troops were sent in. Rand appointed over 800 officers and soldiers despite government orders to take religious sentiments into account; the measures used included entry into private homes, stripping and examination of residents (including women) by British officers in public, evacuation to hospitals and segregation camps, and preventing movement out of the city. Some of these officers have also damaged buildings and sacred objects. The people of Pune viewed these actions as oppressive, and Rand disregarded their protests.

On June 22, 1897, the Diamond Jubilee of Queen Victoria's coronation, Rand and Lt. Ayerst, his military escort, were shot as they were leaving the festivities at Government House. Ayerst passed away immediately, and Rand died from his injuries on July 3. In addition to being accused of the murders in various capacities, the Chapekar brothers and two other people (Mahadev Ranade and Khando Vishnu Sathe) were also accused of shooting two informants and making an attempt to shoot a police officer. All three brothers were found guilty and executed by hanging; a fourth brother, who was still a schoolboy at the time, was given a ten-year harsh jail sentence.

From the Left: Damodar Chapekar, Balkrishna Chapekar, Vasudeo Chapekar

A Humble Family Background...

Vinayak Chapekar, the grandfather of the boys, was the patriarch of a large family that included their parents, Dwarka and Hari, as well as about twenty additional relatives, including six uncles, two aunts, and two grandparents. When Damodar was born in 1869, the family was affluent because they had previously generated lakhs of rupees in revenue. The family's financial situation declined over time, primarily as a result of Vinayak Chapekar's independent nature, which prevented him from submitting to government duty, and his numerous unsuccessful business endeavours. When Damodar Hari was a young kid, the family travelled to Kashi with a group of 25 pilgrims at one point, along with two servants and three carts. The boys also had an older sister, but regrettably, she passed away during the same journey in the modern-day province of Gwalior.

Hari, the father of the Chapekar brothers that we know, attended Poona High School until the sixth standard. After that, a 'Shastri' was assigned to teach him Sanskrit at home so that he might become a kirtankar (a devotional singer who recites a sacred text or story). The brothers of Hari Chapekar were educated to play musical instruments so that they could perform with him. Given the position and age of the family, the decision of Hari to become a kirtankar was met with criticism by the members of his caste and acquaintances. The profession was despised by Vinayak Hari's brothers as well, who left, left the family, and went their separate ways. Even Vinayak Chapekar, who had a skilled "Balbodh" and "Modhi" hand, departed the house for the then-Maratha cities of Indore and Dhar. He then began to beg on the streets, stopped speaking all other languages save Sanskrit, dressed carelessly, and avoided social interaction as much as possible. The family's other members were also struggling with poverty and were compelled to eat in soup kitchens.

Hari Chapekar passed away and was cremated on the banks of the Kshipra; his family was in Nagpur at the time, but regretfully they were unable to travel to Nagpur to attend the funeral. The deceased widow of Hari Chapekar was also by herself. Only one of Hari's brothers remained in their family house as the other brothers all went their separate ways. But when he was alive, Hari taught his children to sing kirtans, and the Chapekar brothers eventually rose to prominence as prolific and well-known kirtankaars. Hari did not have the money to employ professional musicians to play alongside him during his kirtan. The father and kids had mastered their craft and were well-respected for it.

The onset of the bubonic plague and the subsequent horrific atrocities...

A pandemic spread throughout the Bombay presidency towards the end of 1896, affecting residents in Bombay and the nearby towns of Pune. The then-British Raj made major, war-like measures to stop the spread of the plague after it emerged as a threat and started to spread like a summer bushfire. A month later, a considerable chunk of Pune's population had perished from the plague, and almost half of the city's residents had fled to avoid suffering and demise.

Under the leadership of W.C. Rand, an ICS officer who had received administrative work training at a specialised London institution designed for administrative work in India, the Governor of Bombay established 'The Plague Committee'. Rand was assigned to Pune, its suburb, and the cantonment area as a Special Officer. The Governor's directive was that actions should be handled seriously without endangering the beliefs or practises of the Muslim and Hindu communities within Pune's territorial jurisdiction. Under the governor's directive, only female community members would be investigated as part of the plague eradication programme.

Major Paget of the Durham Light Infantry (DLI) seized charge of the officers and soldiers on March 12th, both British and native. They had to go to every region of the city and take the necessary actions to stop the disease from spreading as part of their responsibility. In actuality, they went against the governor's orders and ordered the male members to specific locations to interrogate the family members, including the ladies. Gate-crashing into private homes, interrogating residents, forcing women to remove their clothing, evacuating people to hospitals and segregation camps against their will, removing and destroying personal property - including idols - restraining people from leaving the city, conducting funerals in designated cremation areas, among other inhumane acts - were all examples of their actions. Additionally, if the orders are broken, the subjects risk prosecution.

The Committee completed its report on the Pune Plague on May 19, 1897. *"It is a matter of great satisfaction to the members of the Plague Committee that no credible complaint that the modesty of a woman had been intentionally insulted was made either to themselves or to the officers under whom the troops worked"*, W.C. Rand wrote in his report to the Governor after mentioning that the estimated total plague mortality was 2091.

Numerous well-known persons complained to Rand about the troops' barbarous behaviour before the report was even presented. Rand ignored them, and nothing was done to stop the soldiers. On the Poona Plague, a fictitious report was created. The story was a clear misrepresentation of the facts. The truth is that in the guise of containing the outbreak, Hindu women's modesty was offended in plain sight. According to reports, one of the two Indian ladies who had been raped committed suicide. Blasphemous actions, such as tossing Hindu idols out of the Puja room and other priceless items, allegedly took place with impunity.

Rand was accused of being the cause of the fury among the whole Hindu community in Pune. "The government should not have entrusted the execution of this order to a suspicious, sullen, and tyrannical officer like Rand", Lokmanya Bal Gangadhar Tilak stated in a letter to the Queen. In the interim, there were denials and cynical remarks about the community's lack of participation, etc.

The Plot, and the Action...!

The Chapekars brothers - Damodar, Balkrishna, and Vasudeo, who grew up in Chinchwad, close to Pune, were individuals with a patriotic outlook. As ardent Hindus, they were quite concerned about how the faith had been denigrated and criticised in the name of change. They held the British responsible for their lack of consideration for the religious beliefs of the Indian people. They established a group named *"The Society for the Removal of Obstacles to the Hindu Religion"* and trained some individuals military-style to protect the religion. The Chapekar brothers had long observed the British Sahibs and their behaviour; dissatisfaction over their prejudiced treatment of Indian people was evident on their faces. The Chapekar brothers grew enraged in March 1897 when the forces (DLF) under Major Paget's command caught their attention. No rational military personnel would descend to such a low state as to strip the women in full front of the public and violate their modesty in the name of eradicating the plague. The peevish and irate Rand was blamed by the DLF for this maniacal action. The brothers came together and decided to get rid of Rand at all costs. They also carefully planned how they would kill him in front of everyone.

They had a golden opportunity on a silver platter. The brothers preferred the 22 June 1897 Diamond Jubilee of Queen Victoria's coronation in Pune, according to Damodar Hari Chapekar's autobiography. The rationale was straightforward: Damodar Hari Chapekar thought that the jubilee celebrations at the Government House would draw a sizable crowd of Europeans, including officials of various ranks, providing an ideal opportunity for Rand's murder. The brothers Damodar and Balkrishna chose a location behind a yellow bungalow on Ganeshkhind Road (now known as Senapati Bapat Road in Pune). They would have the necessary view from the vantage point to aim at Rand. The brothers each had a sword and a pistol with them. Another tool in Balkrishna's kit was a hatchet. It was already dark when they arrived at the Government House around 7:30 p.m., at Ganeshkhind. It was a great celebration with several exciting events at Government House. The security was unconcerned by their movements while carrying swords and hatchets; they stashed them for later use beneath a stone culvert close to the bungalow. Damodar waited outside the Government House gate as decided by the brothers, and Rand's carriage pulled up 10 to 15 paces behind it. Damodar signalled for Balkrishna to act when the carriage arrived at the yellow bungalow with the phrase *"Gondya ala re (Gondya has come)"*. The idea was that Damodar would soon join him, and the two of them would shoot Rand to death. Damodar Hari Chapekar unlocked the carriage flap, raised it, and fired a shot. Things went according to plan because Rand's carriage continued to go forward while Balkrishna fell behind. Balkrishna developed misgivings about the people in the carriage after his own. He immediately opened fire at Lt. Ayerst, who was leading Rand's military guard. Ayerst, who was riding in the second carriage, passed away instantly. Rand passed away on July 3, 1897, at the David Sassoon Hospital.

The Aftermath – Arrests and the Persecutions...

As a result of the assassinations, which shocked the British Empire, special officers were quickly appointed to look into the case. The British government announced a reward of 20,000 Rupees for anyone with information regarding the whereabouts of the assassins, who had added a colourful chapter to the history of India's freedom campaign. To instil fear in the hearts of the populace, the police turned to brutal repression. Insinuating stories were published by the Anglo-Indian press, especially The Times of India, in which it was claimed that Lokmanya Tilak's remarks had inspired the murderers to kill Mr Rand and that the Pune Brahmins had plotted to topple the British administration.

In the interim, Damodar Chapekar had been detained in Bombay on suspicion of killing Rand. Chapekar accepted full responsibility for the killing. When people learned of his bold testimony in court, they were astounded. Damodar received a death sentence after being found guilty in the Sessions Court on March 2nd, 1898. Tilak was housed in another wing of the Yerwada prison, while Damodar Chapekar was put in the ward for inmates who would be executed. Damodar Chapekar asked the prison officials for permission to meet Tilak at least once, and they complied with his request. When Damodar first met Tilak, he asked him for a copy of the Bhagavad Gita and demanded that his final rites be conducted as per Hindu traditions. Tilak gave Damodar a copy of the Bhagavad Gita, and when he was being hanged, Damodar remained silent while holding the holy book. As per the deceased's desires, Tilak set up the funeral and last rituals.

In December 1898, Balkrishna Chapekar was taken into custody. The Dravid brothers, who were once friends with the Chapekar brothers, turned informants, and the police were able to apprehend Damodar and Balkrishna Chapekar as a result of the information they provided. On February 8th, 1899, Vasudeo Chapekar, the youngest of the Chapekar brothers and Mahadev Ranade, shot the Dravid brothers outside of their home in Sadashiv Peth, Poona. The following day, the Dravid brothers died as a result of their wounds, while Ranade and Vasudeo Chapekar were taken into custody.

Vasudeo, his brother Balkrishna, and Mahadeo Ranade were all hung at the Yervada prison during the second week of May 1899. The three brothers did not show any signs of guilt or fear as they mounted the gallows since they all believed they were dying for a just cause. Despite being married, there were no problems. The three brothers made a supreme sacrifice that was unlike any other and inspired awe in the hearts of the populace. The three brothers and their friend Ranade, who had sacrificed their lives for the honour of their motherland, were given final rites by Tilak.

The prevailing global media focused on this shocking murder in colonial India committed directly under the control of the Crown, which subtly revealed the darker aspects of the oppressive and tyrannical regime. It damaged the British reputation around the world and exposed their continuous misgovernance and exploitation of Indians, which was no different from the misgovernance during the authority of the East India Company. The New York Times and the Sydney Morning Herald were the prominent ones to cover the incidents in detail.

The Invincible Legacy...

The Chapekar brothers' murder of Rand was not widely perceived as a crime. Lala Lajpat Rai himself praised the freedom warriors Damodar Hari Chapekar, along with his brothers Balkrishna and Vasudeo. Lala Lajpat Rai stated, *"The Chapekar brothers, who killed the two officers who had become unruly during the Poona plague epidemic, were not viewed as criminals by the general populace. The Chapekar brothers bravely accepted their fate. Though they did not respect the act itself, people did admire the motivation behind it. The revolutionary movement in India was actually started by the Chapekar brothers".*

The Chapekars and Mahadev Ranade were hung to death for the murders of Rand and Lt. Ayerst. The account of how these courageous men gave their lives for the sake of freedom is moving. Today, one would think that Rand and Ayerst's deaths were pointless and that Chapekar and Ranade's actions were all childish. But one must keep in mind that they did all of this effort out of love for their nation. The Chapekar brothers had no expectation of financial reward or recognition for their deeds. For their brothers, they sacrificed their lives. They or their family received no personal gain. *"Are we willing to go to such lengths for the good of our country? Have we taken any action for our nation thus far?"* – Before you criticise the brave brothers and the freedom fighters, try to respond to these questions. In reality, criticising such heroic deeds is like a coward pleading for calm in the face of certain death! Also going to hell would be those who did this! Remember that our countrymen will never forget the sacrifice made by the Chapeker Brothers and Ranade. It is permanently engraved on the Indian's psyche!

Even now, one can't help but be proud of the bravery and sacrifice of these young guys, who were still in their early twenties. This is the only known incident of three brothers making a brave sacrifice for the sake of their nation. Heartfelt Obeisance from my end!

CHAPTER THREE

ALLURI SITARAMA RAJU

25th August 1922, Rajavomangi Village, Andhra Pradesh...

The sun had just risen above the horizon and, a pin-drop silence was haunting the village. There was a daunting quietness in the area. Daunting, yet a peaceful quietness. The locals were terrified, but they were also mesmerized. They were petrified by the raid that had just happened the night before, but deep down inside, there was a sigh of relief in the air for them, as every one of them knew that it was another brutal blow to the British Raj. A few kilometres away, the local Police Station was still burning and a note (in Telugu) was found later on, in the station diary which said,

"Along with Rajavomangi, the Government Facilities in Chintapalli and Krishnadevipeta were also turned to ashes!! We now have 26 muskets, 2,500 rounds of ammunition, six .303 Lee Enfield Rifles and a revolver. We are 500 in number and soon will be more than 5000!! I am, Alluri Sitarama Raju, your Kaal!! Stop me if you can!!!"

In the verdant tapestry of colonial India, where monsoon winds rustled through bamboo groves and ancient traditions echoed in tribal whispers, a storm of defiance brewed. The years 1922-24 witnessed the Rampa Rebellion, a chapter in Indian history woven with the courage of the Koya tribe and the indomitable spirit of Alluri Sitarama Raju, their Maanyam Veerudu ('Tiger of the Jungle'). The seeds of rebellion were sown with the draconian Madras Forest Act of 1882. This colonial decree declared Koya ancestral lands, their 'podu' cultivation grounds, as "reserved forests", outlawing their way of life and plunging them into poverty and despair. Hunger gnawed at their bellies, resentment simmered in their eyes, and whispers of resistance danced on the monsoon wind. Enter Alluri Sitarama

Raju, a young sanyasi who had absorbed the Koya spirit, their stories of valour etched in his heart. He embraced the role of leader, transforming from a seeker of truth into Maanyam Veerudu – the Tiger of the Jungle. With a band of loyal tribesmen, honed by the rhythm of the forest and fueled by righteous anger, he launched a series of audacious attacks on British camps.

The Rampa Rebellion wasn't a clash of open battlefields; it was a symphony of guerilla warfare conducted under the emerald canopy. Their movements were phantoms, swift and silent, striking like cobras and disappearing into the dense foliage. Ambushes sprung from hidden pathways, traps lay camouflaged in the undergrowth, and surprise attacks rained down from the whispering bamboo. The Raj, accustomed to bludgeoning force, faltered in the face of this elusive enemy. Raju knew the jungle like the lines on his palm, its secret streams offering water, its hidden caves promising refuge. He used this knowledge to his advantage, outsmarting them with cunning tactics and unwavering courage.

Alluri Sitarama Raju commanded his troops in the Rampa rebellion of 1922, against the British colonial overlords to drive them out of the Eastern Ghats region of the former Madras Presidency. He oversaw multiple raids on imperial police stations throughout the uprising to obtain weapons for his ill-prepared soldiers. Following every raid, he would drop a handwritten note, signed by himself, notifying the police of the specifics of his loot, including the weapons he had taken, and daring them to stop him if they could. Police stations in and near areas of Annavaram, Addateegala, Chintapalle, Dammanapalli, Krishnadevipeta, Rampachodavaram, Rajavommangi, and Narsipatnam were also attacked by his forces, which resulted in severe police casualties.

But the British wouldn't relent. They deployed spies, their whispers slithering through the jungle like venomous snakes. They offered hefty rewards, gold glittering like a mirage in the desert of poverty, hoping to lure betrayers from within the Koya ranks. They even resorted to playing the tribes against each other, poisoning the wellsprings of unity with the venom of suspicion.

The pressure mounted on Raju. His band dwindled the weight of responsibility etched lines on his young face. Yet, he remained the oak tree amidst the storm, his roots deep in the soil of his people's love. He knew the whispers of the jungle, the rhythm of the wind, the warnings of betrayal, and the inevitable end.

Alluri Sitarama Raju

The Birth, and The Awakening of the Tiger...

Alluri Venkata Ramaraju, a free-spirited man with a great sense of patriotism for his motherland with Koya blood coursing through his veins, was married to Suryanarayanamma, a pious lady who was a homemaker and generous by nature. Venkata Ramaraju was a professional photographer, who had seen and captured the dreadful deeds of the British, throughout his professional life. After a while, he settled in the town of Rajamahendravaram (present-day Andhra Pradesh) for vocational purposes. Soon after, on 4th July 1897, Venkata and Suryanarayanamma gave birth to a magnanimous child and they named him 'Rama Raju'. Venkata Ramaraju was a man with immense self-respect, who always strived hard to imbibe the values of independence and freedom in the mind of young Ramaraju. He also once had scolded & humbled a young Ramaraju for adhering to the then-dominant tradition of Indians saluting Europeans as a sign of respect for their superiority.

Alluri Sitarama Raju's childhood was a unique blend of idyllic rural life, cultural immersion, and the awakening of a revolutionary spirit. It was a time of learning, growth, and forging the foundation for the legend he would become. But, just 8 years after Ramaraju's birth in 1905, Venkata Ramaraju passed away and that proved to be a turning point for the young Ramaraju. From a very young age, he started following the footsteps of his father and developed a sharp intellect and emotional maturity. Immersed in the Koya way of life, Ramaraju imbibed their traditions, language, and dances. He learned the secrets of the Rampa hills, forging a deep connection with his ancestral land. He witnessed the impact of the Madras Forest Act, which declared their ancestral lands "reserved forests", destroying their way of life and fueling his simmering anger. He witnessed the hunger, despair, and resentment simmering among his people, and the stories of their ancestors' resistance fueled his determination. The hardship and suffering inflicted by the British Raj on his community ignited a spark of defiance within him. Even as a young boy, he displayed acts of defiance, like refusing to wear badges with King George's picture as a symbol of servitude.

After completing his elementary schooling, Ramaraju enrolled at a High School in Kakinada, where he befriended Madduri Annapurnaiah (1899-1954), who later became a well-known Indian revolutionary as well. In keeping with his reserved and contemplative disposition, Ramaraju considered obtaining Sanyasa while he was in his teens. He relocated to his mother's hometown of Visakhapatnam when he was 15 years old to complete his high school and college studies. He had registered for the fourth form test at Mrs. A.V.N. College there. During his time there, he frequently travelled to remote parts of the Visakhapatnam region to become acquainted with the hardships faced by the local tribal population. At this time, he made a wealthy man's acquaintance and fell in love with Sita, the friend's sister, whose premature death devastated him. To keep her memory permanent, Ramaraju then appended her name to his and came to be generally known as Sitarama Raju. Eventually, he stopped attending school without finishing his course. In this case, Sitarama Raju was taken to Narasapur by his uncle Rama Krishnam Raju, a "tehsildar" in the West Godavari district, who also taught him while he was growing up. Raju was then admitted into the nearby Taylor High School. He eventually abandoned conventional schooling, though, and studied Telugu, Sanskrit, Hindi, and English literature on his own. Despite having no special schooling, he had a keen interest in astrology, herbal medicine, palmistry, and equestrianism. At the age of 18, he became a Sanyasi or a religious ascetic.

The Draconian Law, and Raju...

Alluri Sitarama Raju's life was largely impacted by the Madras Forest Act of 1882, which turned the picture-perfect story of his early years into a sombre tale of suffering and disobedience. It was more than just an official order; it was a barbed wire fence set up around the Koya way of life, a subtle but oppressive force that profoundly influenced Sitarama's future. In its icy, bureaucratic jargon, the decree designated the verdant slopes of Rampa, the Koya tribe's traditional homeland, as "reserved forests". This harmless-sounding word belied a terrible truth. Traditional Koya 'podu' cropping, a long-standing sustainable form of slash-and-burn farming, was forbidden. Their primary food source was ruled off-limits because it didn't fit the colonial idea of "scientific forestry". This was an attack on the Koya people's soul, not just an administrative annoyance. Their relationship with the land was spiritual, cultural, and ancestral in addition to being economic. Beyond being a place to eat, the forest served as their playground, pharmacy, and shrine. This holy pact was effectively broken by the act, casting them apart and adrift. For Raju, a small youngster at the time, the effect was instantaneous and profound. He observed his people's eyes clouded with despair and their cheeks marked with hunger. He heard the murmurs of unhappiness evolve into snarls of rage as families were driven off their ancestral grounds and into desolate government townships. The formerly bustling Koya villages turned into barren wastelands. This was a narrative that Raju had internalised, not only something he had heard from others. The harshness of the incident also affected his family. The property where their ancestors had raised food and fostered dreams for generations was designated as "reserved". Injustice hurt more than just in their minds; it left them with a gnawing emptiness in their stomachs and a persistent fear for the future.

Raju, however, was not one to take the injustice lying down. He thought that the key to breaking free from the oppressive bonds of colonialism was education. He left the Rampa highlands and went to Rajamahendravaram's classroom halls to seek education, but the inflexibility of classrooms broke his soul. More audible than ink-stained papers were the whispering bamboo and rustling leaves. His meanderings across the Rampa highlands transformed into an exploration pilgrimage. He discovered the land's mysteries, including the roads that eluded the colonists' blind eyes, the caves that offered safety, and the secret streams that slaked thirst. Now, he was more than just a sanyasi; he was taking in the spirit of his people, their suffering, their pride, their smouldering rage. The Madras Forest Act turned out to be the spark that lit his inner fire. It was a personal insult, a declaration of war against his people, his culture, and his existence, not merely a legal order. He could not watch in silence as the misery it caused. He needed to be their spokesperson and protector.

As a result, the deed wasn't merely a minor incident in Raju's life; rather, it served as the furnace where his character was formed. It influenced his core beliefs, methods, and motivations. It served as a continual reminder of the injustice he opposed and the driving force behind his unyielding opposition. He was adamant about tearing down the barbed wire fence - not just for his people, but also for justice and freedom. There is more to the tale of Alluri Sitarama Raju and the Madras Forest Act than just a youngster and a statute. It's a symbol of the human spirit's resilience and refusal to be defeated, serving as a microcosm of the greater fight against colonial oppression. It serves as a reminder that when the spark of resistance burns for a just cause, in the heart of a Tiger of the Jungle, no amount of strict legislation can put it out!

Evolution of a Leader and Becoming the 'Maanyam Veerudu'...

During his high school years, Raju would frequently go on horseback rides with his uncle to remote hill locations. This allowed him to become acquainted with the range of issues that the many tribal people facing British colonial rule were dealing with at the time. Having a strong devotion to pilgrimage, he travelled to Nashik and Gangotri in 1921, the birthplace of the sacred rivers Godavari and Ganga. In Chittagong, he met several revolutionaries while visiting the nation. He was deeply horrified by the socioeconomic circumstances of the Indian population, especially that of the tribal people, and decided to launch a campaign to free them from British domination. Subsequently, he made his home in the Papi hills, which are close to Godavari District and have a large population of tribal people.

To elevate his moral stature, Alluri Sitarama Raju first became a Sadhu and engaged in a variety of spiritual practices. He also developed into a skilled herbal healer. He was particularly irritated by the Christian missionaries' attempts to convert the hill tribes during this period since he considered conversion as a means of advancing imperialism. He went on to lead an ascetic life among the indigenous people, needing only the necessities. With his blessings, he would return much of what was donated to him to the tribal people, taking only food items such as fruits and honey. His captivating personality quickly earned him a reputation among the tribe as someone endowed with supernatural abilities, even a messianic status. This reputation was reinforced by the myths he made up about himself as well as the ones he accepted from others, such as the one about his unstoppable nature. The hill tribes were peaceful but fierce people who had to pay high fees for simple tasks like gathering fruit and fuel, grazing livestock, and engaging in trade with strangers. It was against the law for them to cultivate in the "Podu" or "Jungle", and their extremely old way of life was endangered. Raju pleaded with the officials for forgiveness after seeing their exploitation, but his pleas were in vain. At that point, he believed that revolt was the only option left.

After taking note of the tribespeople's complaints and resolving their issues, he began organising them, teaching them about their rights, and getting them ready to fight against the tyranny and oppression of the forest and revenue authorities, missionaries, and the police. He learned a great deal about the geological features while exploring the forest regions, which aided him later on as a guerilla warfare tactician. During this period, when their ancestral properties were seized by the British, two liberation-fighting Koya tribal brothers, Gam Malludora and Gam Gantamdora, joined Raju's army and were made lieutenants. Raju emerged as the group's natural leader as the harsh British methods grew intolerable and revolt became their last chance to live in freedom. Then, in an attempt to win him over, the Government offered him 60 acres of lush land for his ashram; nevertheless, he turned it down and stuck up for the people. Thus, sparked the rebellion, which blossomed into a revolution with a gigantic roar from the 'Tiger' who sent shivers down the spine of the Raj!

The Rampa Revolution (1922-24)...

History whispers of rebellions, and flickers of defiance against the established order. But sometimes, these sparks ignite, growing into roaring flames of revolution that reshape the world. The transition from rebellion to revolution is a fascinating dance, where the ground shifts beneath the feet of empires, and the whispers of discontent morph into the thunderous chorus of change. At its heart, a rebellion is a localized cry of anguish, a clenched fist against specific injustices. It might be a village rising against oppressive taxes, students protesting stifling regulations, or a marginalized group demanding their rightful place in the sun. These uprisings are often spontaneous, fueled by immediate concerns and lacking a grand ideological vision. They may flicker brightly for a time but often lack the sustained momentum or strategic direction to overthrow existing power structures. But in the crucible of struggle, a rebellion can evolve into something far more potent - a revolution. This metamorphosis happens when the whispers of discontent gather into a symphony of voices, united by a shared vision of a better future. The parochial concerns broaden, encompassing not just specific injustices, but the very foundations of the existing order. The fight for tax relief becomes a fight for self-determination, the protest against student restrictions becomes a demand for intellectual freedom, and the struggle for recognition morphs into a battle for equality and justice. This shift in focus requires organization, a unifying ideology that binds disparate voices into a cohesive force. Leaders emerge, not just charismatic figures, but strategists who can navigate the treacherous terrain of resistance, formulate plans, and mobilize resources. They articulate the aspirations of the masses, weaving the threads of discontent into a tapestry of revolution. A revolution, even if it fails to achieve its immediate goals, can leave an indelible mark on the world. It can become a catalyst for change, and a source of inspiration for future generations. Its ideals may echo through history, influencing political discourse, shaping social movements, and serving as a constant reminder of the human spirit's yearning for a better world.

Now, the Madras Forest Act of 1882 brought about reforms that meant the locals would starve to death. Their main way of escaping this fate was to work as coolies - demeaning, hard, exploitative, foreign workers, for the government and its contractors on projects like building roads. The ancient hereditary position of the "muttadars", who up until that point had served as the de facto rulers in the hills and tax collectors for the Rajas (Local Kings) who lived in the plains, had also been emasculated by the British Raj authorities at the same time as the Act. Now these persons were reduced to the status of regular public officials, with no right to inherit their post, no capacity to charge taxes at will, and no sweeping powers. As a result, rather than being at odds with one another, the tax collectors and cultivators were now generally in favour of the colonial authority. Raju utilised the unhappiness of the tribal people to bolster his anti-colonial fervour, while simultaneously catering to the complaints of muttadars who shared his cause instead of those who were self-serving in their quest for a restored status for themselves. According to this, the majority of his supporters were drawn from the tribal groups, but there were also notable members of the muttadar class who had previously taken advantage of them, even though many of them were still undecided about fighting for what Raju believed to be the greater good.

Raju used elements of the Non-Cooperation movement (which was launched in 1922, by M.K. Gandhi) to win over the public. These included advocating for 'Khaddar', temperance, an anti-alcohol campaign, and a boycott of colonial courts in favour of panchayat courts. Although he was instrumental in spreading some of the movement's techniques among the hill people to increase their political consciousness and desire for change, the movement had already spread to the plains by the time it died out in early 1922. Because of these actions, now he was placed under police surveillance starting in February 1922. However, neither the movement nor the British political establishment appear to have taken notice of the fact that he was using his propaganda as a cover to incite an armed uprising. Even though he was occasionally observed applauding Gandhi, Raju actively pushed the Adivasis to arm themselves and become knowledgeable about guerilla tactics.

The turning point arrived in August 1922. Driven by the desperation of his people and the fire of righteous anger, Raju led a series of audacious attacks on British police stations. These weren't pitched battles fought on open fields; they were symphonies of guerilla warfare conducted under the emerald canopy. Koya warriors, their movements blending with the rustling bamboo, used their knowledge of the terrain to launch surprise attacks, disappear into the dense foliage, and leave the British reeling in confusion. With the help of his allies, Raju amassed a formidable army of combatants. All of the Raju's men wore only Khadi uniforms, thanks to the assistance of Rallapalli Kasannla, a non-cooperator and producer of Khadi from Tuni. It was said that Raju was a frequent wearer of Khadi. The revolutionaries used conventional weapons like spears, bows and arrows, as well as communication strategies like banging drums and blowing whistles to communicate with one another. Initially, they had amazing success fighting the British. Since the British were well-armed with contemporary rifles and would not be deterred by traditional armament, Raju decided that the best course of action would be to remove the British from the enemy and begin attacking their police posts.

Raju led a group of 500 people in a raid and looting of the police stations in Rajavomangi, Krishnadevipeta, and Chintapalli between August 22 and 24, 1922. From the seizure, he was able to take control of several weapons, including one revolver, six .303 Lee Enfield rifles, 2,500 rounds of ammunition, and 26 muskets. After that, he went around the region recruiting new members and murdering a policeman who was part of a team ordered to track him down. One defining feature of these raids had been Raju's practice of signing a written note in the station logbook detailing the loot he had taken, including the weapons he had taken, the day and hour of his attack, and his challenge to the police to stop him if they could! Raju had given his followers strict orders to attack only the foreign enemy and not any Indian combatants. His subordinates had been so meticulous in following the instructions that they had released the Indians and only attacked the foreign troops when a mixed force of Europeans and Indians marched along winding mountain roads. But the fight wasn't just about military tactics. Raju also understood the power of propaganda very well. He played upon the Koya's rich folklore, weaving tales of heroic ancestors who defied colonial oppression. He used symbols - a white flag with a red tiger, a stark reminder of their resistance - to rally support and spread fear among the British. His message resonated, echoing through the valleys and carrying on the wind, igniting a spark of defiance in hearts far beyond the Rampa hills. The unknown terrain made it difficult for the British to pursue Raju, and the locals in the sparsely populated areas were eager to help Raju instead of being unwilling to aid them, even if it meant giving him shelter and intelligence. Initially, the core group of rebels were about 80-100 while they were based in the hills, but when they decided to take action against the British, the number of rebels increased significantly due to the participation of villagers.

On September 23, 1922, more casualties were inflicted on the Britishers when Raju's troops assaulted a police party passing through the Dammanapalli Ghat from a strategic location, killing two policemen and solidifying his image among the irate populace. In September, there were two more successful attacks against the police. The British then brought in men of the Malabar Special Police, who were trained for such operations, realising that Raju's guerilla warfare would require a corresponding response. The British retaliated with brute force. They deployed spies, their whispers slithering through the jungle like venomous snakes. They offered hefty rewards for Raju's capture, gold glittering like a mirage in the desert of poverty, hoping to lure traitors from within the Koya ranks. They even resorted to playing the tribes against each other, poisoning the wellsprings of unity with the venom of suspicion. However, it was unsuccessful in using threats and rewards to get the locals to stop supporting Raju or to inform others about him. Afterwards, police stations at Annavaram, Addateegala, Narsipatnam, and Rampachodavaram were raided. Once, while Raju was worshipping Goddess Kali at Dharakonda, a group of special policemen attempted to attack him but were unable to achieve their goal. After this episode, Raju became more well-known among the tribal people, who began to regard him as having supernatural abilities!

Aggi Raju, a dependable aide whose deeds were deemed heroic, provided Sitarama Raju with excellent support during his raids. Eventually, Assam Rifles unit detachments were sent in to put an end to the unrelenting resistance. The district collectors at the time, Bracken of East Godavari and R.T. Rutherford of Visakhapatnam, who had jurisdiction over the rebel areas, used all available means, both legal and illegal, to put an end to the rebellion and apprehend Alluri Sitarama Raju. These measures included burning villages, destroying crops, killing cattle, and abusing women, but they were all ineffective. J. R. Higgins, the agency commissioner, issued a reward of Rs 10,000 for the head of Rama Raju and Rs 1,000 for each of his lieutenants, Mallam Dora and Ghantam Dora. The battle drew attention from both influential leaders and the general public nationwide for roughly two years. In an attempt to put an end to the "Maanyam" rebellion in April 1924, the British Government then dispatched T. G. Rutherford, who used severe forms of torture and abuse on people to find Raju and his close associates.

The pressure mounted on Raju. His band dwindled the weight of responsibility etched lines on his young face. Yet, he remained the oak tree amidst the storm, his roots deep in the soil of his people's love. He knew the whispers of the jungle, the rhythm of the wind, the warnings of betrayal, and the inevitable end...

Calming the Storm, and leaving behind a Stupendous Legacy!

The transition from rebellion to revolution is not a clear-cut moment; it is a fluid process, a 'dance' between desperation and ambition, organization and chaos. Understanding this complex dynamic requires looking beyond the immediate spark of discontent and examining the broader canvas of societal structures, ideological aspirations, and the unwavering human desire for a just and equitable world. For in the embers of a rebellion, a revolution may flicker, waiting for the right wind to fan it into a transformative blaze that rewrites the very narrative of history.

Raju was gaining most of his support from the plains districts, therefore the British divided the hills and restricted his power to the territories of Darakonda, Gudem, and Peddavalasa. Despite this, he tried to court more people to his side, notably the Congressmen from the plains, but to his great disappointment he found they had little sympathy for him and were against his activities on the pretext that he broke the Gandhian concept of Nonviolence. The Congress leadership's lack of support for Raju and the tribals was actually due to their shared class interest with the moneylenders and Zamindars that Raju and his people were rebelling against. Other political bodies' responses were either unresponsive or unfavourable.

The verdant hills of Rampa, once echoing with the defiant roars of Alluri Sitarama Raju, fell silent in May 1924. His death, a cruel twist in the drama of the Rampa Rebellion, remains a potent symbol of both betrayal and unwavering courage.

While the details of his final days are etched in history, delving deeper reveals a narrative woven with complex threads of loyalty, strategy, and the relentless pursuit of justice. One trusted confidante, driven by personal ambitions and possibly lured by hefty rewards, turned against Raju. In April 1924, this individual revealed the location of Raju's camp, tucked away in the dense forests near Chittiguda village. The information, a poisoned dart aimed at the heart of the rebellion, set in motion a chain of events that would culminate in tragedy. On May 5th, a British force, led by Captain C.W. Russel, descended upon the camp under the cloak of dawn. The surprise attack caught Raju and his men off guard. Though outnumbered and outgunned, the Maanyam Veerudu fought with the ferocity of a cornered beast. The dense forest became a battleground, the rustling leaves and echoing gunshots a grim symphony of defiance and desperation. Despite their valiant efforts, Raju and his men were overwhelmed. One by one, they fell, their sacrifices echoing through the trees. Raju himself, wounded and surrounded, refused to surrender. He fought with the unwavering spirit that had become his legend, his final moments a testament to the cause he championed. The official account claims that Raju was killed in the crossfire, his body riddled with bullets. However, whispers in the Koyyuru village in the Rampa hills tell a different story. They speak of a final stand, of Alluri Sitarama Raju choosing to end his own life rather than face capture and humiliation. Whether he fell to enemy fire or his own hand, the result remained the same: the Tiger of the Jungle had breathed his last!

Ghantam Dora, Raju's lieutenant, was assassinated on June 6, 1924, while his brother Mallam Dora was apprehended and sent to jail. Later, following Indian independence, Mallam Dora was elected to the Lok Sabha in 1952 from the Visakhapatnam constituency. Alluri Sitarama Raju's attempts to wage an armed war against one of the greatest empires without the backing of the state were appropriately acknowledged. He was a formidable tactician in the nearly two-year Guerrilla warfare campaign, which the British administration reluctantly acknowledged, even though it took them more than ?4 million to beat him. News of Raju's death spread like wildfire, a wave of grief and anger washing over the Rampa hills and beyond. The Koya people mourned their leader, their symbol of resistance, their voice against injustice. Yet, amidst the despair, a flicker of defiance remained. Alluri Sitarama Raju's legacy, his spirit of rebellion, and his unwavering commitment to the cause refused to be extinguished. The Rampa Rebellion, though ultimately unsuccessful in achieving its immediate goals, had dealt a significant blow to the British Raj. It exposed the vulnerabilities of colonial rule, highlighted the plight of indigenous communities, and ignited a spark of resistance that would burn bright for years to come.

Raju's death, therefore, was not simply the end of a man's life; it was a turning point in the struggle for freedom. He became a martyr, his sacrifice a rallying cry for many who followed in his footsteps. His story, etched in the memory of the Rampa hills and whispered in the hearts of his people, became a testament to the power of courage, the resilience of the human spirit, and the unwavering pursuit of justice. Even today, Alluri Sitarama Raju remains a revered figure, not just in Rampa but across India. His image adorns walls, his story is told in songs and poems, and his spirit inspires countless people who continue to fight for the rights of the marginalized and oppressed. While the details of his final moments may remain shrouded in a mist of conflicting accounts, the significance of his life and death is undeniable. He lived and died a Tiger of the Jungle, a symbol of resistance against injustice, and his legacy continues to echo through the verdant hills of Rampa, a reminder that even the mightiest empires can fall when faced with the unwavering spirit of a people determined to be free.

CHAPTER FOUR

KHUDIRAM BOSE

Bengal! - not just a geographical entity, but a crucible where the flames of India's freedom struggle burned brightest. Long before the fire of rebellion roared, embers of discontent flickered in the hearts of Bengalis. The 1905 partition, a cruel stroke of the British Raj, sliced their land in two, dividing not just territories but families and communities. This wound festered, birthing a deep resentment that pulsed through every vein of Bengal. In this environment, where anger danced with intellectual ferment, whispers of resistance coalesced into organised cries for freedom. Young men and women, their eyes gleaming with revolutionary fervour, gathered in smoke-filled rooms, their voices hushed but their resolve unshakeable. The air crackled with the electricity of rebellion, fuelled by fiery speeches and revolutionary tracts smuggled in from across the Bay of Bengal. The British, of course, weren't oblivious. Bengal, the thorn in their imperial crown, was under constant surveillance. But even their oppressive might couldn't stifle the spirit of rebellion. From daring assassinations to audacious bombings, the revolutionaries struck fear into the hearts of the colonisers, showcasing their unwavering commitment to the cause. Calcutta, Bengal's beating heart, pulsated with revolutionary zeal. Prestigious institutions like Presidency College became breeding grounds for revolutionary thought, where professors like Aurobindo Ghosh, their voices vibrating with conviction, instilled in their students not just academic knowledge but a burning desire for Swaraj. Young men and women, their hearts brimming with courage, learned the art of guerilla warfare, perfected bomb-making, and honed their skills in the shadows.

Bengal!! The turf of the revolutionaries! The year 1905 in India was not just another year on the calendar. It was a year etched in fire, a year where a map was sliced in two, and the flames of revolution flickered into a roaring inferno. In its arrogance, the British Raj drew a line across Bengal, dividing the land of poets and revolutionaries, and unwittingly ignited a firestorm that would forever alter the course of Indian history. The partition, ostensibly for administrative convenience, was a blatant attempt to weaken Bengal's burgeoning nationalist movement. It separated the Hindu-majority western districts from the Muslim-majority east, creating a fertile ground for communal discord and political manipulation. But the British miscalculated. The partition, instead of fracturing, ignited a sense of unity and outrage that transcended religious boundaries. The partition gave rise to a more radical strain of nationalism - the revolutionaries. Groups like the Jugantar Party and Anushilan Samiti emerged, advocating for armed resistance. They saw the British Raj as an illegitimate occupier, and the partition, as a blatant act of tyranny. Bombings, assassinations, and daring acts of defiance became their weapons, their answer to the injustices inflicted upon their motherland.

One such gem from a relatively small town of Bengal, Midnapore, was Khudiram Bose. In the annals of India's freedom struggle, few names evoke such a bittersweet mix of awe and sorrow as those of Khudiram Bose and Prafulla Kumar Chaki. Their youthful audacity, their unwavering commitment to the anti-colonial cause, and their tragic end at the hands of the British cast a long shadow on the narrative of India's fight for independence. This chapter delves into their story, not merely as a chronicle of a single event, but as a window into the revolutionary zeal that gripped a generation and the complex moral questions that continue to echo through history. Khudiram Bose, barely a teenager when the embers of revolution started to flicker, hailed from Midnapore, Bengal. Orphaned at a young age, he found solace in the teachings of Swami Vivekananda and the burgeoning nationalist movement. Prafulla Chaki, from Bhagalpur, also felt the stirrings of discontent against British rule, fueled by personal experiences of injustice and the fiery rhetoric of leaders like Aurobindo Ghosh. Both, drawn by the magnetism of the cause, found themselves gravitating towards the Jugantar party, a radical wing of the Indian National Congress advocating for armed resistance. The year 1907 proved pivotal. Douglas Kingsford, a British judge notorious for his brutality towards Indian revolutionaries, became a target for the Jugantar. Khudiram, barely 18, and Prafulla, a few years his senior, volunteered for the mission. The plan was audacious and fraught with danger – to assassinate Kingsford in Muzaffarpur...

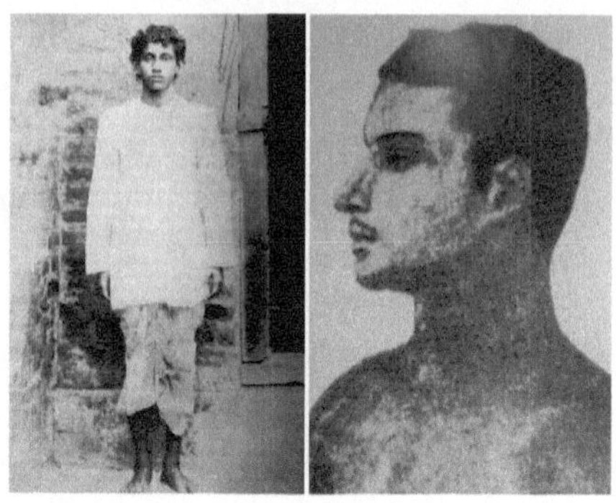

Khudiram Bose and Prafulla Kumar Chaki

Early Beginnings, and laying the foundations...

Born on December 3, 1889, to a Bengali Kayastha family, Khudiram Bose was raised in the undivided Medinipur region of Bengal in the small village of Mohobani, which was within the purview of the Keshpur Police Station. In the Narajole district, his father worked as a Tehsildar. In a household with three daughters, Khudiram was the fourth child. Preceding Khudiram's birth, Trailokyanath Bose and Lakshmipriya Devi gave birth to two boys, both of whom passed away too soon. As per the long-standing traditions of the community, the baby was symbolically given to his elder sister in return for three handfuls of the food grains known as "Khud" in the local region. This was done to prevent the infant from passing away too soon. In this manner, Khudiram became his name! Khudiram's early years were filled with happiness, but sadly, at the age of six, he lost his mother. The next year, his father passed away. His older sister, Aparupa Roy, took him to her home in Hatgachha village, which was under the control of the Daspur Police Station. Aparupa's husband, Amritalal Roy, got him admission to Tamluk Hamilton High School.

The year was 1902-03 and Khudriam was in his teens now. Sri Aurobindo and, at the same time, Sister Nivedita delivered public lectures and private sessions with the different revolutionary groups and secret societies that were solely aimed at eradicating the tyrannical British Raj with a systematic armed revolution by grooming the youth and nurturing them accordingly. These groups looked forward to the Bengal and the adjacent regions of

Bihar, where the discontent for the British was of the highest order amongst the youth. The Jugaantar Party and the Anushilan Samiti, being the top institutions for the cause, caught the attention of young Khudiram and he had also made up his mind to cater to their cause by putting his blood & sweat and working fingers to the bone for the motherland.

As Khudiram grew, India was simmering with the discontent brewed by British rule. The infamous Partition of Bengal in 1905 ignited a wave of nationalistic passion, particularly in Bengal. The fiery speeches of Sri Aurobindo and Sister Nivedita resonated deeply with the young Khudiram, who had now turned 15. He actively participated in anti-British demonstrations, distributing pamphlets and boycotting British goods. At this point, Khudiram Bose shifted his allegiance to Anushilan Samiti and made contact with Barindra Kumar Ghosh's Calcutta network. At the age of 15, he volunteered and was first imprisoned for handing out leaflets criticising British authority in India. Khudiram participated in the detonation of bombs near police stations and targeted government officials while he was just 16 years old.

Across the Hooghly River, in the tranquil town of Rangpur, Prafulla Kumar Chaki navigates a different path towards the same destiny. Though financially well-off, he feels the iron grip of colonial oppression constricting the breath of his nation. The sight of poverty-stricken farmers driven to desperation by harsh British tax regimes fuels his anger. The fiery editorials in newspapers like "Yugantar" become his gospel, stirring his spirit with tales of oppression and rebellion. On December 10, 1888, in a village in the Bogra region of modern-day Bangladesh, which was then a part of the Bengal Presidency, Prafulla Chandra Chaki was born into a prosperous 'Jotedar' family of Bihar. Following the completion of his elementary schooling, he travelled to Rangpur with his older brother Pratap Chandra Chaki, whose father-in-law was well-known in the city. Due to his participation in a student rally that broke East Bengal legislation, he was expelled from Rangpur Zilla School in Class 9. After that, he enrolled in Rangpur National School, where he interacted with revolutionaries and developed a belief in and practised revolutionary ideologies. He enjoyed swimming and riding horses. He was a well-known wrestler and lathikhalowar (stick fighter) in his youth. He discovered solace in the writings of Barindra Ghosh, whose words paint a vivid picture of a free India and a call to arms against the oppressors. Prafulla was introduced to Calcutta by Barin Ghosh, and he joined the Jugantar party. The ideals of the Jugantar Party resonate with Prafulla's yearning for freedom, and he found himself drawn to their clandestine meetings. His sharp intellect and unwavering dedication caught Barindra's eye, and soon, Prafulla was entrusted with tasks of vital importance - procuring supplies, disseminating messages, and recruiting young revolutionaries. Assam and Eastern Bengal's first lieutenant governor, Joseph Bampfylde Fuller, was the target of his first mission: assassination. But the plan never came to pass, and Prafulla Kumar Chaki moved on towards another chapter that was about to be written in the golden annals of Indian History.

The Notorious and The Ever-Atrocious - Douglas Kingsford!...

Judge Douglas Kingsford, was a controversial figure in Colonial India whose brutalities towards Indian revolutionaries and disregard for their basic rights earned him the ire of the nationalist movement. Kingsford was known for giving excessively harsh sentences to those implicated in anti-colonial activities. He frequently imposed terms of life imprisonment or transportation for long periods for offences deemed relatively minor by the Indian public. Such harsh punishments instilled fear and served as a stark deterrent to any dissent against British rule. Accounts from various sources, including memoirs of revolutionaries, mention the inhumane treatment meted out to prisoners under Kingsford's jurisdiction. Physical torture, solitary confinement, and denial of basic amenities were regular practices employed to break the spirit of political dissidents. The Muzaffarpur Central Jail, where he often presided over cases, bore a particularly notorious reputation for its brutal treatment of prisoners.

Kingsford actively participated in suppressing any form of political dissent or expression of nationalism. He banned newspapers and journals deemed critical of the British Raj, stifled public gatherings, and ordered the arrest of individuals suspected of harbouring revolutionary sympathies. This systematic silencing of dissent created an atmosphere of fear and stifled the burgeoning freedom movement. One example is the case of Barindra Ghosh, who was also Khudiram's mentor. Kingsford sentenced him to life imprisonment for his involvement in the Alipore Bomb Case, where bombs were manufactured to target British officials. This case sparked outrage among nationalists, highlighting the perceived disproportionate punishment meted out by Kingsford.

His criticism of Indian nationalists was motivated more by hatred and bias than by any sense of merit. After he rendered inhumane, irrational, and spiteful judgements against the "Swadeshi & anti-Partition activists", he gained a negative reputation and was later viewed as harsh and brutal by people throughout Bengal. A 15-year-old child rebelled against the police who mistreated the Indians in the court during the dramatic trial of Aurobindo Ghosh, editor of Vandemataram, and publisher Bipin Chandra Pal, which Kingsford presided over. Judge Kingsford gave the kid 15 lashes without showing any regret or regard for his age. "Vande Mataram!" was the boy's cry after each lash. Revolutionaries were incensed and enraged by this news, which made the top page of every Bengali daily. The revolutionaries of the Jugantar organisation resolved to kill the horrible Judge Kingsford since they were thoroughly enmeshed in this deed. Numerous news articles regarding the harsh British rule, their conceit towards the locals, and their lack of regard for their idea of a free India could be found in Vandemataram, Yugantar, and other journals, that were run by the local patriots and revolutionaries. He was a well-known antagonist of Indians and a harsh critic of the Bengali daily Jugantar.

Hemchandra Kanungo, a revolutionary who learned how to make bombs from Europe, attempted to assassinate Kingsford for the first time with a book bomb. An empty tin of Cadbury cocoa was packed with a pound of picric acid and three detonators. Paresh Mallick, the young revolutionary, placed this into a hollowed-out piece of Herbert Broom's Commentaries on the Common Law and covered it in brown paper to send to Kingsford's home. Kingsford put the sealed parcel on his shelf for a later inspection. In March 1908, the government moved the judge to Muzaffarpur, Bihar, and upgraded him to the rank of District Judge out of concern for his safety. His bookshelf, library, and furniture all vanished with him.

A Destiny Forged in Fire: Khudiram Bose meets Prafulla Kumar Chaki

The year is 1907. Bengal, the heartland of India, throbs with the pulsating rhythm of a nation awakening. The embers of discontent against British rule, fanned by the Partition of Bengal, have ignited a fire of nationalism that burns brightest in the hearts of young men like Khudiram Bose and Prafulla Kumar Chaki. Though their paths will soon converge, their journeys to the crossroads of destiny unfold separately, each marked by its unique trails of fire and resilience. One fateful day, Barindra brings Khudiram and Prafulla together. The meeting takes place in a dimly lit room, the air thick with anticipation and the scent of revolution. Barindra lays out the audacious plan - to assassinate Douglas Kingsford, the ruthless District Magistrate of Muzaffarpur, whose brutality towards revolutionaries has become a symbol of colonial tyranny. The mission requires two volunteers, two souls willing to walk the tightrope between life and death, and two flames ready to merge into a single inferno of defiance. Khudiram's eyes gleam with a dangerous ardour. The prospect of striking a blow at the heart of British power electrifies him. Prafulla, his face etched with steely resolve, nods in unwavering agreement. In that shared gaze, across the flickering lamplight, a bond is forged – a bond not of blood, but of shared ideals, unwavering courage, and a willingness to sacrifice everything for the sake of freedom. The meeting is brief and devoid of unnecessary sentimentality. Barindra outlines the plan, detailing the route, the target, and the escape route. Khudiram and Prafulla listen intently, absorbing every detail like water-parched land. Questions are asked, plans are meticulously reviewed, and then, a tense silence descends upon the room. The die is cast. Their paths have converged, their destinies intertwined, and together, they will walk the precipice of history, their names forever etched in the annals of India's fight for freedom.

The meeting concludes with a silent handshake, a shared nod of acknowledgement. As Khudiram and Prafulla step out into the night, the air crackles with a sense of imminent danger and electrifying excitement. They are no longer boys playing war games. They are revolutionaries, instruments of vengeance, and harbingers of change. The road ahead is fraught with peril, the outcome uncertain, but their hearts burn with an unwavering conviction – they will strike a blow for their motherland, even if it costs them their lives. They walk away, not as boys playing at revolution, but as men steeled by the fire of commitment, their hearts ablaze with a love for their nation that burns brighter than any fear of death.

The path ahead is fraught with peril, the outcome shrouded in uncertainty. Yet, as they disappear into the shadows, the faint whisper of a revolutionary anthem rises from their lips, a defiant melody that carries the promise of a free India and a testament to the unwavering spirit of two young men who dared to dream and fight. Anushilan Samiti, on the other hand, were also totally persistent in their attempt to kill Kingsford. A reconnaissance team comprising Prafulla Chaki and two other men visited

Muzaffarpur in April. The bomb, which consisted of a black powder fuse, a detonator, and six ounces of dynamite, was given by Hemchandra upon their return. Prafulla Chaki and Khudiram Bose now returned to Muzaffarpur.

A Night of Fire & Fate: Muzaffarpur Assassination & the Escape Attempt...

The air hangs heavy with a premonition of change as Khudiram and Prafulla, barely a man and a boy, leave behind the cloak of darkness and head towards the outskirts of Muzaffarpur. Armed with crude bombs crafted from iron pipes and filled with explosives, their hearts pound with desperate hope and unwavering resolve. Their target, Kingsford, embodies the tyranny they seek to shatter, his face forever etched in their minds as the face of oppression. But, suspicion was aroused by Aurobindo Ghosh, Barindra Ghosh, and their associates' actions. The intentions for Kingsford's life were discovered by the Calcutta police. The Superintendent of Police at Muzzafarpur disregarded the warnings from Commissioner F.L. Halliday. But the magistrate's house was to be guarded by four men. Meanwhile, Kishorimohan Bandyopadhyay ran a benevolent Dharamshala, where Khudiram Bose and Prafulla Chaki took up the names 'Haren Sarkar' and 'Dinesh Chandra Roy', respectively. Over the following few days, the two kept an eye on their target's regular activities. The two rebels were able to keep their identities a secret for more than three weeks. The Calcutta CID officer came back with a letter stating that the two had not shown up, from Armstrong, the Superintendent of Muzaffarpur.

Khudiram was in place to carry out his plans with Prafulla on that fateful evening of April 29. Acting like schoolboys, they looked over the Muzaffarpur Park, which is across from The British Club and is used by Kingsford. Regretfully, a police officer saw them. A British barrister named Pringle Kennedy had a daughter and wife who were playing bridge with Kingsford and his spouse. They decided to return home at about 7:30 p.m. The carriage that held Kennedy and his family was the same one that Kingsford and his wife rode in. Khudiram and Prafulla ran towards their carriage and hurled the bombs inside as soon as they arrived at the eastern gate of the European Club's compound. After a tremendous explosion, the carriage was brought to Kingsford's residence.

Chaos erupts in the wake of the blast. The carriage, mangled and smouldering, lies on the side of the road, the victims within mangled by the shrapnel and consumed by the fire. Prafulla and Khudiram chose separate routes to avoid being apprehended. At dawn, Khudiram had covered about 40 kilometres (or 25 miles) on foot and arrived at a station known (then) as "Waini". At a tea shop, two armed constables, Fateh Singh and Sheo Pershad Singh, approached him as he requested a glass of water. Upon noticing his tired and sweaty demeanour, along with his dirty feet, the officers assumed something was wrong. They decided to hold Khudiram after growing increasingly suspicious after asking him a few questions. Immediately after Khudiram engaged in combat with the two men, one of the two concealed revolvers came loose. One of the constables grabbed Khudiram from behind like a bear hug before he could bring the second one down on them. Khudiram, who was considerably younger and had less muscle, was unable to defend himself or flee. A train map, a sheet from the rail timetable, thirty rupees in cash, and thirty rounds of ammunition were discovered on his person. Khudiram's destiny was set in stone! Prafulla, on the other hand, had journeyed for many long hours. A youthful vehicle was approaching Trigunacharan Ghosh, a civil servant, about lunchtime. Knowing about the explosion of the bomb, he concluded that Prafulla was the other revolutionary. In an attempt to preserve his life, Ghosh allowed him to eat, sleep, and take a bath in his home. That same evening, he made plans for Prafulla to go back to Kolkata. From Samastipur, he caught a train to Mokamaghat, and from there, he continued to Howrah. Nandalal Bannerjee, a sub-inspector with the Indian Imperial Police, was riding in the same compartment. After striking up a discussion, he discovered Prafulla to be the other revolutionary. Bannerjee dispatched a message to the police station in Muzaffarpur when Prafulla descended at the Shipwright station to take a sip of water. Banerjee tried to detain Prafulla at the Mokamaghat station. Prafulla attempted to use his handgun to fight his way through, but ultimately, with one remaining bullet, he murmured 'Vande Mataram' and shot himself in the mouth. And that was it! That was it!!! That's how a young, ardent and zealous Prafulla Kumar Chaki entered the gates of heaven - free and prideful!!

'A Young Grandeur' - The Historical Trials and Martyrdom of Khudiram Bose

"The Railway station was crowded to see the boy. A mere boy of 18 or 19 years old, who looked quite determined. He came out of a first-class compartment and walked all the way to the phaeton, kept for him outside, like a cheerful boy who knows no anxiety.....on taking his seat the boy cheerfully cried Vande Mataram". - The Statesman, 2nd May 1908

Khudiram was transported to Muzaffarpur in handcuffs on May 1. Everybody in the community flocked to the police station to see the teenage lad who was surrounded by armed officers. Khudiram was led to the house of the district magistrate, Mr. Woodman. Khudiram was required to make a declaration or statement to the magistrate. He accepted full responsibility for the murder, not realising Prafulla had passed away. It was not until Khudiram concluded his statement that Prafulla's body arrived in Muzaffarpur. Khudiram knew that lying would not accomplish anything. He recognised Prafulla's body, and the British also got information from the interaction with sub-inspector Bannerjee. Ultimately, the British colonial authorities did not believe Khudiram, and they conspired to detach Prafulla's head from his corpse and send it to Calcutta for better confirmation, and that's what they did eventually!

The First Hearing...

Judge Corndoff, together with jurors Nathuni Prasad and Janak Prasad, oversaw the historic trial which began on May 21, 1908. Khudiram Bose and Prafulla Chaki were housed in Mrityunjay Chakraborty's Dharmashala by Mr Kishorimohan Bandopadhyay, who was also tried for aiding the revolutionaries in their objective. The trial of Kishorimohan was divided from that of Khudiram after Mrityunjay passed away during the trial. The British colonial government's prosecutors were Mannum and Binod Bihari Majumdar. Khudiram was defended by attorneys Kalidas Basu, Upendranath Sen, and Kshetranath Bandopadhyay. Later in the trial, Kulkamal Sen, Nagendra Lal Lahiri, and Satischandra Chakraborty joined them; none received payment for their legal services. Khudiram resubmitted his statement to Magistrate E.W. Bredhowd on May 23, in which he denied any responsibility or involvement in any part of the mission and operation up until the explosion. Khudiram was first hesitant to sign this statement, but his solicitors convinced him to do so. The court and the prosecution got an anonymous letter of warning on June 13, the day the verdict and sentencing were supposed to be delivered. It informed them that they had one more bomb coming from Kolkata and that moving forward, the Biharis, not the Bengalis, would be the ones to end their ugly lives! However, the fact that the letter demonstrated that Khudiram might not have been the only planner or executor of the Muzaffarpur bombing, along with Khudiram's advanced age, should have given the judge an alternative sentence other than death, which gave the defence attorneys more comfort. However, to everyone's dismay, the judge gave Khudiram the death penalty.

Khudiram responded with a quick, involuntary smile. Startled, the judge questioned Khudiram about whether he had comprehended the significance of the given sentence. In response, Khudiram said he had for sure. In front of a crowded courtroom, Khudiram boldly said, grinning, *"If I could have some more time, I could teach the judge how to make bombs!"* in response to the judge's follow-up question. By that point, the judge had given the police instructions to lead the boy out of the courtroom.

Khudiram has seven days under the law to file an appeal with the High Court. Khudiram refused to appeal. But after being convinced by his counsellors that he would live to serve his country after being freed and would have age on his side if he was given a life sentence rather than being hanged as a result of this appeal, Khudiram eventually agreed, coldly, to accompany his defence team.

The Second Hearing, and the Sentence...

The hearing before the High Court was held on July 8, 1908. To save a young man who had suddenly emerged as a national hero and wonder, Narendrakumar Basu came to Khudiram's aid and focused all of his legal knowledge and expertise on this issue. He contested the session court's decision, claiming that it was faulty and not in line with the law. In addition, Khudiram was not informed of the accused's identity or position during the initial statement, he reasoned, and by article 164 of the penal code, the accused must present his testimony before a first-class magistrate, which Mr Woodman was not. Second, as Basu pointed out, article 364 mandates that all inquiries made of the accused be made in Bengali (the person's mother tongue), and that all of the accused's responses in that language be confirmed in writing. However, in Khudiram's case, this was done in English. Moreover, Khudiram's signature was supposed to be given on the statement on the same date and at the time of the statement in the presence of the magistrate, but in actuality, Khudiram was made to sign the day after, and in front of a different person, who was an auxiliary magistrate. Last but not least, there was no evidence that Khudiram was permitted to make a free statement without any direct or indirect coercion following his apprehension, as such a statement is by definition supposed to be entirely voluntary, with the magistrate being certain that it was so. In addition, Prafulla, also known as "Dinesh" (the name used in the trial) was the bomb specialist and stronger than Khudiram, according to Narendrakumar Basu. Therefore, it's very possible that "Dinesh" was the one who threw the bomb. Moreover, Prafulla's suicide while facing arrest only serves to support the theory that he was the bomb thrower in the first place. After the defence, it was stated by the two British judges that the final verdict would be passed on 13 July 1908. But the British justices upheld the judgement and gave Khudiram Bose a death sentence by hanging on 11th August, even though Narendrakumar Basu's reasoning in the court was sound enough to spare the life of an 18-year-old!

On August 11, the area surrounding the prison began to fill up well in advance of the appointed hour of six in the morning. Individuals carrying floral garlands occupied the front rows of the assembly. Near Khudiram, lawyer-journalist Upendranath Sen of the Bengali news daily "Bengali" reports arriving at the scene by 5 AM in a car equipped with all the required clothing and funeral preparations. Following the hanging, police officers lined the main thoroughfare to keep back the throng as the funeral procession passed through the city. As the carriage went by, the crowd continued tossing flowers at Khudiram's body and the whole region was shell-shocked by the roars of *"Khudiram Amar Rahe!!!"*

An Eternal Legacy!

"Khudiram's End: Died cheerful and smiling"... *"Khudiram's execution took place at 6 a.m. this morning. He walked to the gallows firmly and cheerfully and even smiled when the cap was drawn over his head".* - Amar Bazaar Patrika, 12th August 1908...

"Khudiram Bose was executed this morning... It is alleged that he mounted the scaffold with his body erect. He was cheerful and smiling". - The Empire, 12th August 1908...

"Neither the Jubilee murder of 1897, nor the reported tampering of the Sikh regiments had produced so much commotion, and the English public opinion seems inclined to regard the birth of the bomb in India as the most extraordinary event since the mutiny at 1857" - Kesari, 26th May 1908...

Following his martyrdom, Khudiram gained so much popularity that Bengali weavers began creating a unique style of dhoti with the word

"Khudiram" printed on one side. These dhotis were worn by boys pursuing their education at colleges as they stitched and marched towards independence. Khudiram's greatest legacy lies in his embodiment of revolutionary defiance against British colonialism. In an era marked by rampant oppression and the snuffing out of dissent, he dared to raise his voice, albeit through explosive means. The attempt on Kingsford's life, however flawed in its execution, symbolized a bold rejection of colonial authority and a refusal to bow down to tyranny. His act, though unsuccessful in its immediate objective, resonated throughout India, injecting a potent dose of courage and inspiring others to challenge the seemingly unassailable might of the Raj.

Khudiram's execution cemented his status as a martyr for the cause of Indian freedom. His unwavering resolve in the face of death, his refusal to plead for mercy, and his defiant words – *"Vande Mataram! Long live Mother India!"* – became rallying cries for countless revolutionaries. His hanging at the young age of 18 fueled public outrage and galvanized the freedom movement, highlighting the brutal cost of colonial oppression and the lengths patriots were willing to go to for their nation's liberation. The unintended tragedy of the Muzaffarpur bombing also throws light on the often-overlooked dilemmas faced by revolutionaries operating in clandestine movements. While Khudiram's act ignited a fire of defiance, it also highlighted the risk of civilian casualties in armed struggle, an ethical minefield that continues to plague revolutionary movements. Examining his legacy necessitates a nuanced understanding of his actions within the complex historical context of colonial India. However, Khudiram's legacy is not solely one of martyrdom. Examining his life beyond the Muzaffarpur incident reveals a young man of remarkable intellect, unwavering dedication to the national cause, and a keen awareness of the complex realities of his time. He actively participated in anti-colonial activities, distributed revolutionary pamphlets, and underwent rigorous training in bomb-making, demonstrating a commitment that went beyond impulsive action.

Khudiram's legacy transcends the borders of India, finding resonance in other struggles against colonialism and tyranny across the globe. His story resonates with young people fighting for justice and freedom in various corners of the world, serving as a testament to the timeless spirit of rebellion and the universal yearning for self-determination. Khudiram Bose's legacy is not simply a static monument carved in stone, but a living flame that continues to flicker within the hearts of Indians and people fighting for freedom worldwide. His defiance, his sacrifice, and his unwavering commitment to a free India continue to inspire, challenge, and compel us to confront the complexities of history and the relentless pursuit of justice.

45

CHAPTER FIVE

SWATANTRAVEER VINAYAK DAMODAR SAVARKAR

Vinayak Damodar Savarkar - Some individuals find great inspiration in these three words, while others immediately label him a bigot, a coward, or a fanatic to put an end to the discussion.

"Savarkar is not a person, he is an idea. The unity of identity (reconciliation) in mind, word and deed, as manifested by Savarkar in his life, is unique, it is supernatural. His personality, his work, his oratory and his poetry give such a dimension to the life of Savarkar that he will always be remembered in the history of the world. Whenever one will fight against subjugation, jump into the battlefield against injustice, whenever the time for the sacrifice of life comes, whenever the moment of surrendering everything and regaining the lost freedom of the motherland will be present, Savarkar's name will be remembered with an immense proud which would infuse strength in the minds of generations!" – Atal Behari Vajpayee, 28th May 2006, Pune.

He was the kind of man that, love him or hate him, you simply couldn't ignore. He was an exceptionally talented student from the start of his academic career. He was born on May 28, 1883, in the little hamlet of Bhagur, in the Maharashtra region of Nashik. He had an older brother, a younger brother, and a younger sister as he was the middle child. Young Vinayak was drawn to the feeling of patriotism from a very young age, which was also reflected in his daily life at the time. He was a well-read student with a strong interest in History and Culture. His aptitude for writing and public speaking, as well as his capacity for persuasion, all proudly exhibited his fervent patriotism! Savarkar was an avid reader who was familiar with nearly all of the Western thinkers. For his classmates to be inspired by revolutionary literature, he would even transcribe it from English into Marathi. Let's not forget that he lost a lot of family members when he was incarcerated. Due to his arrest, he had to stay away from his wife and kids because they were being shunned by society.

An Interesting Anecdote!...

Savarkar had a remarkable oratory talent. This first became apparent when he was only 10 years old and competing in an extempore competition while still in school. Although the judges incorrectly claimed that he had by-hearted the topic and that his pragmatic approach wasn't used, as required in an extempore, he outsmarted everyone in the competition. He issued a challenge to everyone, incensed by the outcomes, to make another speech on any subject the judges would suggest. In under 5 minutes, he gave an equally exciting speech that was met with a standing ovation from the audience. Now, why was this particular anecdote included in the discussion? Because it demonstrates Vinayak's incredible dedication from a young age and how brilliantly he used his brains! (This trait of his was frequently displayed in his final years).

Vinayak Damodar Savarkar

Abhinav Bharat: Beginning of a New Era...

Young Vinayak was greatly influenced by his older brother, Ganesh Damodar Savarkar (also known as Babarao Savarkar), and together they launched "Mitra Mela" in 1899. While Savarkar was a good student at the esteemed Ferguson College in Pune, he renamed it, "Abhinav Bharat", in 1904 in a meeting attended by roughly 200 members from various places in Maharashtra, taking it after Giuseppe Mazzini's Young Italy. After Savarkar left India to study law in 1906, the organisation expanded to include several ardent revolutionaries and political activists and had sections in various parts of India and London. Savarkar quickly joined 'India House', another secret club in London that had already been founded by Shyamji Krishna Verma. Savarkar, who published a book on the subject in 1909, was the first Indian to formally recognise the "Sepoy Mutiny of 1857" as the "War of Independence." Because it was difficult to publish this book in England, he smuggled the manuscript to the Netherlands, where it was eventually published. Savarkar was one of the most prominent figures to oppose the terrible Morley-Minto reforms from abroad when they were passed in India at the time.

Swiftly identifying Savarkar as a significant "threat" to their imperial dominion, the British made him a political prisoner. Savarkar was detained in London in 1910 and given a warrant for his extradition to India due to his associations with the revolutionary organisation India House.

While the ship was anchored in the port of Marseilles on the way back to India, Savarkar made a valiant attempt to flee and seek refuge in France. In violation of international law, the French port officials however returned him to the British government. Savarkar was transferred to the Cellular Jail in the Andaman and Nicobar Islands after being convicted of two life terms of incarceration totalling 50 years upon his return to India. Vinayak, who was then 27 years old, was subjected to horrifying torment that would eventually affect him forever (rather, changed his approach to fighting the war against the British).

The Torturous Cellular Jail...

The Port Blair Cellular Jail was purposefully built to operate like a machine, robbing inmates of their humanity through cruel punishment and, it would seem, "reforms." The British Government made sure that the political prisoners stayed separated from one another, which had the desired effect of solitary confinement.

Savarkar wrote an autobiographical book titled "My Transportation for Life" in which he detailed his time spent in such a cellular prison. The inmates' regular work assignments included turning the oil mill. They felt as though they were being yoked like animals to the handle that rotated the wheel because this one piece of work was so brutal and inhumane. Any type of human being may lose all of their vitality and, it would seem, their spirit in just 20 spins of that savage wheel. Additionally, regardless of age, every prisoner received the same treatment. Vinayak's older brother Ganesh Savarkar was also a prisoner at the cellular jail during the time Vinayak was serving his sentence there. Savarkar describes the emotional suffering, torment, and PTSD (Post Traumatic Stress Disorder) his brother experienced as a result of the physical labour (or "reforming," as they called it!) while in the cellular jail, in chapter 9 of My Transportation for Life.

Authors Cathy Scott-Clark and Adrian Levy published "Survivors of our Hell," an article in The Guardian in 2001, in which they both discovered some secret documents from the Andaman cellular jail. One of the infamous tales they disseminated concerned a prisoner by the name of Mahavir Singh who went on a hunger strike to protest the use of corporal punishment while incarcerated. The authorities attempted to forcefully feed him by inserting a rubber catheter into his nostril to end the strike! However, as a result of it puncturing his lungs, he was "drowned with milk," which led to pneumonia and finally took his life. Furthermore, they stated that "in just a 3-4 year period, 3500 out of 8000 detainees had either been slain or perished as a result of the cruel treatment that was administered to them". Later, the British Government was forced to admit that the cellular jail's death rate had surpassed 30% by the 1930s.

Mr Barrie (an Irish), the jailor of the Andaman Cellular Jail later admitted that Savarkar frequently served as the leader of several of the prisoners' work strikes. In the Andaman Islands, Savarkar was identified as the "father of the turmoil." Revolutionaries were maligned and mistreated by Barrie. He cruelly tormented and viciously mistreated the detainees. They were in a terrible state when Savarkar came, but he somehow made things better for inmates in general and political prisoners in particular. Savarkar committed to protecting the rights of political prisoners and to compel the jail administration to provide them with physical and cultural facilities, which included a demand for a properly maintained library (to preserve the inmates' sanity and effectively reform them!). Savarkar's leadership during these work strikes demonstrated his unwavering nationalist spirit and dedication to his causes, even in the face of extreme hardship. As a result, he was sent to the Ratnagiri Jail in the year 1921 (on May 2) and eventually freed in the year 1924.

The Cellular Jail in Port Blair: Where Savarkar Spent 10 Solitary Years
(Credits: Rediff.com)

Revolution via Social Reformation, and Hindutva!...

Savarkar was an atheist who did not believe in a specific God in the traditional sense; this fact is not widely known. Those who don't know (or, I suppose, don't care) accuse Savarkar of being a religious extremist and fomenting "hatred" among the populace. However, there are several records and proofs to the contrary. Rejecting casteism, Veer Savarkar held that people are "graded" according to their "karma" rather than their place of birth. He wrote *"Jatyuchchedak Nibandh" (Essays on abolition of caste)* and *"Vidnyan Nishtha Nibandh" (Essays on Scientific Temper)* while incarcerated in Ratnagiri. In his play *"Ushaap" (Antidote to a Curse)*, he addresses issues such as untouchability, the kidnapping of women, Shuddhi & Vratabandha, and the hypocrisy of conservatives. On particular occasions, such as temple entries, he wrote poems *("Malaa devaache darshan gheu dya", i.e. Let me pray)*.

"The Essentials of Hindutva" is a book by Savarkar that some people have misconstrued to the point where they believe Savarkar solely wants Hindus (Brahmins) to live in India! The following are some of the profound

topics he discussed in his work that demand careful clarification:

Listed by Savarkar as the 7 "shackles" of Indian society are as follows:

First, Savarkar says that the rigid caste system "deserves to be thrown into the dustbins of history." Veer Savarkar's second change was to make Vedic literature more accessible to all people, not just members of a specific caste. He described Vedic literature as India's one-of-a-kind contribution to humanity and civilizational wisdom for the entire human race. The third was to encourage people to pursue any vocation of their choosing based on aptitude and ability and to end rigidity based on caste. Savarkar argued that "merely imitating what one's father accomplished, will make one both complacent and unproductive" in the absence of desire, competition, or aptitude.

Fourthly, Savarkar was a proponent of international travel and the idea that Indians should leave the country to explore other countries to "bring back the best of the world and spread the fragrance of India and her culture to every corner of the globe." Fifth, Savarkar wished to eliminate the ban on dining with people of different castes. "Religion is in the heart, soul, and spirit; not the stomach," he had declared.

The promotion of the sixth was that of inter-caste marriages. Veer Savarkar emphasised the necessity to cultivate a scientific temperament as the seventh component. We are 200 years behind Europe, he said, adding that industrialization, technology, and contemporary ideas could ensure that every man and woman in India has a job to do, food to eat, clothes to wear, and a pleasant life to live. Additionally, Savarkar organised the Shuddhi, or purification or conversion, of those who had defected from the Hindu faith as a result of threats and coercion. He organised a bonfire for the Statue of Untouchability on February 22, 1933, to much hoopla. He provided Dr Ambedkar with support throughout his anti-untouchability campaigns in Mahad and Nashik.

Misconceptions about Hindutva...

Savarkar carefully outlined the idea of Hinduism in his work "The Essentials of Hindutva." To further their political goals and engage in their dirty politics, several people and a few political parties have misappropriated these concepts on a bigger scale.

One: "Muslims should be boycotted" - This is the most widespread myth of them all, yet Veer Savarkar doesn't say anywhere in his book that Hindus should despise Muslims and force them to leave the country.

Two, "Hindu Rashtra" - The four Vedas, a collection of shlokas and hymns that essentially emphasise how one should live one's life, are the foundation and spirit of Hinduism. Additionally, the word "Hindu" comes from "Sindhu" or "Sapt-Sindhu," which means the region of the river's seven tributaries, including the Sindhu or Indus. Therefore, rather than only referring to a religious identity and "sanctimonious dogmas," the name "Hindu" refers to a cultural identity and way of life.

Three, "Savarkar promoted the Brahmanical Patriarchy" - As was made clear in the previous section, Savarkar did not support the hereditary caste system and organised numerous ceremonies for all societal groups to provide them with the immense knowledge of the Vedic and Pauranik scriptures, which are already deeply ingrained in our cultural identity. Additionally, he frequently showed his unwavering support for Babasaheb Ambedkar's stance against prejudice towards the untouchables.

Four, "Savarkar was the brainchild of the two-nation idea" - Few people are aware that Sir Syed Ahmed Khan, the founder of AMU and a close ally of the British, first proposed the Two-Nation theory in 1878, before Savarkar was even born. In reality, Savarkar vehemently opposed it and spoke of a terrible consequence should the country be split along religious lines.

Myths and Refutations about Vinayak Damodar Savarkar...

To KNOW what Savarkar did is easy, but to UNDERSTAND what Savarkar did and intended to do in the near future is exactly what people have highly misunderstood. Time and again, Savarkar has been deliberately misinterpreted and portrayed as a coward, a broken man and a 'Maafiveer' instead of a 'Swatantraveer'! Many people who claim to be the torch-bearers of peace, love and non-violence have been blotting the image of Vinayak Damodar Savarkar and his entire family, just so that Savarkar's grand aura, his ideas and his fiery persona would outcast their freedom 'fighters'. Nonetheless, several major accusations have been brought against this fearless individual throughout the years.

Before we proceed ahead, we have to understand the clear difference between a Petition and an Apology. A petition is a formal request for action, typically addressed to a government official or public entity. An apology is a way to show respect for someone's feelings, value their friendship, and be honest and humble. A petition can include requests to dismiss a case, reduce bail, or provide a continuance. A petition can also be used to appeal a court's decision. An apology can include three elements: Acknowledgement of wrongdoing, Expressing regret, and Making a promise to act differently in the future.

Accusation 1:

SAVARKAR WROTE APOLOGIES AND MERCIFUL LETTERS TO THE BRITISH WHEN HE WAS IN KAALA PAANI!

Rebuttal Points:

Veer Savarkar wanted to renew the fight (for independence) after escaping the British clasps.

Veer Savarkar himself revealed in his memoirs that he had often petitioned the British for his release (from Andaman jail), but that he had never expressed regret for his acts (against the British) in any of his pleas. Since Savarkar was a barrister, there was nothing improper in trying to get Savarkar's release through the channels of then-current British law. According to him, it was every revolutionary's responsibility to continue attempting to flee the British and revive the revolution. He used to share this opinion with the other prisoners who were revolutionaries regularly.

The renowned revolutionary Sachindranath Sanyal provides proof of this. The Lahore conspiracy case had resulted in a life sentence for him. Similar to Savarkar, he was freed on the condition of good conduct but was later sentenced to life in jail once more - this time for being the driving force behind the Kakori case. *"Savarkar had also promised cooperation (with the British government) like me"*, says Sachchndranath in his book. *"I was released but not Savarkar. Why? Because the government feared that if Savarkar was released there may be another round of revolutionary upsurge in Maharashtra" (Pg. 226, 'Bandijeevan').*

Veer Savarkar's petitions included substance that was part of his long-term plan to fight British power!

In 1913, before presenting a petition to Sir Reginald Craddock, the Home Secretary of India at the time, Savarkar had a brief conversation with him. In transmitting the document to the British Government, Sir Cradodck made it quite evident that "It cannot be said to express any regret or repentance". A hardline revolution against a tyrannical, suppressive and mighty empire can only be kept alive when the revolutionaries have a safe space away from the clutches of the authorities of that empire. This is a very fundamental thing to understand and a similar thing had happened in the past - when Chhatrapati Shivaji Maharaj was imprisoned by Aurangzeb in Agra, he had played a similar sort of politics to return to his base (Sahyadri) and continued the fight for Hindavi Swaraj (Kindly take a note that I'm not comparing the two personalities. I'm comparing the two situations).

Hence, on a similar note, Savarkar had a grand strategy of uniting people against the British and for that only reason, he had written multiple petitions to the British. Furthermore, Savarkar's aims are unequivocally revealed by the autobiographies of other notable revolutionaries who were also Savarkar's fellow prisoners, including Ullaskar Dutt, Bhai Paramanand, Pruthvi Singh Azad, and Ramcharan Sharma.

Accusation 2:

SAVARKAR DID NOT HAVE TO UNDERGO ANY SEVERE HARDSHIPS IN THE JAIL!

Rebuttal Points:

Although limited, the documents discovered in Andaman jail and the autobiographies of fellow revolutionaries attest to the harsh treatment that Savarkar endured.

Pruthvi Singh Azad, who was also undergoing a jail term (at Andaman) between 1916 and 1921 writes, *"Veer Savarkar had taught the youth of modern India the lesson of revolution. He was one of the brightest leaders of the youth with a revolutionary bent of mind. The British made such a powerful personality to do the work of bullocks. He was forced to produce thirty pounds of oil per day in the oil mill"* (*'Kranti ke Pathik'*, page 108).

Now, during the Japanese occupation (Second World War), a large portion of the Andaman jail's records were lost. But according to the jail documents that are currently accessible, Savarkar received the following harsh punishments:

- On July 15, 1911, the eleventh day after being admitted to the jail, he was placed in a cell for six months of solitary confinement.
- Beginning on August 16, 1911, he was shackled to an oil mill (much like a bullock) for 14 days.
- His confinement had ended on January 15, 1912. However, on June 11, 1912, he was sent back to solitary confinement for a month after it was discovered that he had some paperwork.
- He was put through seven days of 'khadi bedi' beginning on September 19, 1912, after it was discovered that he had written a letter to another prisoner (In 'khadi bedi', a prisoner wears handcuffs that are fixed high up in a wall, requiring them to remain upright until they are released from punishment).
- Again, starting on November 23, 1912, a month of solitary incarceration for the same conduct.

In addition, Savarkar stated in his autobiography that he endured many penalties and difficulties that were illegal and hence not documented in the records; this is a point that is supported by the memoirs of other fellow prisoners who were revolutionaries. Thus, despite their incompleteness, the records that are now accessible provide some insight into the severe penalties and adversities he endured.

Veer Savarkar's unwavering will and mental fortitude are well demonstrated by the experiences related to other revolutionaries!

Ullaskar Dutt had been subjected to such cruel treatment in the cellular jail that he had temporarily lost his mental balance. Before that, when he was being held in shackles, he had a hallucination in which he saw jailor David Barry challenge him to a wrestling contest. Savarkar accepted the challenge on Dutt's behalf and won! (*"Twelve Years in Prison", pages 64 and 65)* This occurrence happened in the year 1912. Now, it is evident that up until that point (1912), Savarkar must have radiated a strong will to fight and a steady mentality since even during a condition of hallucination, Savarkar was the one who seemed deserving of fighting on Ullaskar Dutt's behalf.

Because he participated in a strike, jail personnel threatened to extend the term of another prisoner, Ramsharan Sharma, in 1913. According to reports, he said, *"If Savarkar can serve 50 years in prison, then even I can serve the longer sentence"* (*'Kala Panika Aitihasik Dastavej', page 53)*. This demonstrates that Savarkar was still viewed as the ideal by the other incarcerated revolutionaries in 1913. Could it have happened if Savarkar had lost his mind and given up? In his autobiography "Apbeeti", the great revolutionary Bhai Paramanand, who was incarcerated for his involvement in a 1919 strike, states that jailor Barry and the jail administration would hold the Savarkar brothers accountable for any disputes that occurred in the jail between the inmates and the administration.

Accusation 3:

AFTER BEING RELEASED FROM ANDAMAN, SAVARKAR DID NOTHING FOR THE NATION. ALSO, HE 'HELPED' THE BRITISH AND LATER ON, HE OPPOSED SUBHASH CHANDRA BOSE!

Rebuttal Points:

Savarkar's outstanding efforts to end untouchability and the accounts of other outstanding modern leaders:

During the 14 years of his protracted house confinement at Ratnagiri, Savarkar was prohibited from engaging in any political activity. Thus, he started campaigns to end the unjust behaviours associated with the caste system, untouchability, and blind faith that were then common in Hindu culture. Following his incredible efforts to end untouchability, Vithal Ramji Shinde declared in public, "May God grant Savarkar the years I have left to live!" Dr Ambedkar had expressed his satisfaction that Savarkar was one of the few notable figures of the day who thought the caste system ought to be abolished.

It is unnecessary to repeat what has already been stated and written about Savarkar's significant contribution to the public domain's eradication of untouchability. It is sufficient to argue that many notable modern (social and political) figures, including M.K. Gandhi, would not have made the arduous journey to Ratnagiri to visit Savarkar if he had been working with the British.

To stop the partition of the country, Savarkar launched a mass awakening movement.

After 1937, Savarkar was permitted to take part in political events. He rose to the position of Hindu Mahasabha President. The prospect of partition was very real because of the Muslim League's irrational demands and the Congress's appeasement strategy towards them. Savarkar started a movement of mass awakening to stop partition. In his speech on (Singapore) radio, Rashbehari Bose said "I consider it my duty to pay my respects to a senior freedom fighter colleague like you. You have yet again displayed your great statesmanship by proposing that India's foreign policy should not be dependant on that of any other country and our enemy's enemy should be our friend".

Eulogy (Tribute) offered by Subhash Chandra Bose and Rashbehari Bose to Veer Savarkar:

Netaji Subhash Chandra Bose stated in his speech on Azad Hind Radio that it is encouraging to see Savarkar boldly encouraging Indian youth to enlist in the (then British) army, while the Congress leaders are choosing to mock them as mercenaries because of their irrational and unwise decisions. We at the Indian National Army (INA) have trained soldiers because of Savarkar's efforts.

It is now possible to prove beyond a shadow of a doubt that Savarkar communicated with Rashbehari Bose. It's also evident from this evidence that Rashbehari Bose supported Savarkar's campaign to get young Indians to enlist in the army. The biography of Savarkar was written by Rashbehari Bose and published in the Japanese magazine 'Dai Ajia Shugi' in late March and early April. It had the title *"Savarkar – Work and personality of the rising leader of New India"*. Additionally, Rashbehari Bose once said, "One would feel politically empowered only if one (understands and) agrees with Savarkar's views". So, Savarkar certainly holds a special place among the greatest Indian freedom fighters.

Accusation 4:

SAVARKAR WAS IN FAVOUR OF THE TWO-NATION THEORY

Rebuttal Points:

It wasn't pioneered by Savarkar in the first place!

Sir Syed Ahmed originally put out the two-nation idea in 1878. It was further supported by the famous Urdu poet Muhammad Iqbal. Later, it was embraced by the Muslim League, led by Jinnah, as a demand for partition. Savarkar's numerous remarks make it abundantly evident that he was unrelated to these happenings.

Savarkar had urged the Hindu Mahasabha activists (who were his followers) to oppose the nation's partition:

Savarkar highlighted that he was being mistakenly portrayed as the creator of the two-nation idea by purposefully misrepresenting his entire views as stated in an interview with the daily 'Kaal' (published on August 19, 1943). Savarkar further stated, "Basically, Muslims all over the world, have always considered themselves to be a separate religious nation under the leadership of the Caliph (the Caliphate). However, in reality, Hindus by themselves constitute a nation from the perspective of a (modern) political democracy. They are in the majority and have been inhabiting this country from time immemorial. Muslims, on the other hand, are an aggressive minority". Savarkar had always urged his supporters to resist the impending partition of India brought about by the Muslim community's (aggressive) stance.

One more accusation was thrown on Vinayak Damodar Savarkar and with the help of this accusation, many politicians have maintained their filthy political prowess over the years. The accusation is that Savarkar was involved in the assassination of M.K. Gandhi. The court had then fully cleared Savarkar of this accusation due to the lack of any corroborative evidence. Now, it is accurate to say that Nathuram Godse was once a follower of Savarkar. But once, Savarkar resigned from the presidentship of the Hindu Mahasabha in 1946, Godse and others were not in touch with Savarkar at all.

Later on, a **'Kapur Commission'** was established to re-open the case of Gandhi's assassination which did try to paint Savarkar as one of the guilty in the plot to kill Gandhi. Certain individuals even went so far as to claim that Savarkar's bodyguard Appa Kasar and secretary Gajanan Damle had admitted before the Kapur commission that they knew Savarkar was involved in the (Gandhi) murder plot. In actuality, though, neither Kasar nor Damle ever gave a testimony before the panel, even though their testimonies had already been recorded by the Bombay police on March 4, 1948. They were not called as witnesses in the case of the killing of Gandhi. Among the 101 witnesses the Kapur Commission looked at, their names are NOT on the list.

Recently in 2018, the Supreme Court of India dismissed the conclusions that were drawn on Savarkar in the Kapur Commission and stated that *"The submission of the petitioner that Shri Savarkar has been held guilty for the murder of Gandhiji is misplaced!'"*

The Final Word....

Vinayak Damodar Savarkar, Subhash Chandra Bose, Lala Lajpat Rai, Lokmanya Bal Gangadhar Tilak and many other gems were there who worked fingers to the bone for India's freedom instead of just spinning a wheel and burning down clothes. Savarkar in his last few years had crumbled mentally, and emotionally. "I gave my entire life to my nation, and all I'm getting is this???!" Isn't it obvious that his conscience might have felt it after a point in his life? Yamunabai, Savarkar's wife, passed away on November 8th, 1963. Savarkar quit medications, food, and water, which he called atmaarpan (fast until death) on February 1st, 1966. In an article titled "Atmahatya Nahi Atmaarpan", which he published before passing away, he made the case that it is preferable to terminate one's life on one's terms rather than waiting till one dies when one's life's purpose has been fulfilled and one is no longer able to benefit society. Savarkar had urged his family to perform his burial solely and forgo the customs associated with the 10th and 13th days of the Hindu calendar before he passed away. Well, many people also labelled him a "coward" when he requested pardon to leave the Andaman jail, despite his vision for his country's feelings.

But this supposedly "liberal" society ignores the fact that to defeat foreign invaders, you must unite on all fronts, whether they be political, military, or social (the latter being the most important, especially for a nation like India). Savarkar made a determined effort to bring Indians together on a societal level in his later years, despite being released on the condition that he does not get involved in politics. This also demonstrated his "never give up" attitude from his early years (thus the extempore narrative in the first section of "An Interesting Anecdote"), as well as his unwavering ambition to work for the welfare of his nation.

In the end, a few fundamental queries come up: Did we truly comprehend Savarkar? Did we truly make an effort to uphold his legacy? Are we paying him justice and making an effort to draw from his solid ideas and efforts to forge our national identity? Many have argued that Vinayak Damodar Savarkar ought to have received the prestigious Bharat

Ratna award, but regardless of whether he does or not, he is far above any accolade, and I believe that our society as a whole will truly pay tribute to him by learning from and compassionately acting upon his righteous conscience.

CHAPTER SIX

MADANLAL DHINGRA

1906, India House, Highgate, London...

A mist clung to the cobbled streets, shrouding the imposing Victorian houses in an aura of mystery. Inside India House, on a quiet side street, a different kind of fog swirled - one charged with revolutionary keenness and whispered dreams of freedom. Tonight, two souls destined to etch their names in the annals of Indian history were about to cross paths: the fiery orator, Vinayak Damodar Savarkar, and the young firebrand, Madanlal Dhingra. Savarkar paced the dimly lit room, his restless energy casting shifting shadows on the worn Persian rug. His sharp features, a hawk's beak of a nose and intense, burning eyes, mirrored the turmoil within. Already a controversial figure in India exiled for his incendiary writings, he had found purpose in London, the heart of the very empire he sought to dislodge. India House, a haven for like-minded revolutionaries, served as his pulpit, his arsenal the spoken word, laced with defiance and the intoxicating dream of an independent India. Tonight, the room buzzed with the hushed murmur of conspirators. Pamphlets with inflammatory titles like "The Cult of Bomb" lay scattered on tables, their bold fonts screaming unspoken rebellion. Young men, their faces etched with a yearning for liberation, sipped chai and debated revolutionary tactics. Then, Madanlal Dhingra entered. Tall and slender, with a youthful flush on his cheeks, he carried a quiet intensity that belied his 23 years. Unlike the others, his dress was neither ostentatious nor bohemian; he retained an air of privileged upbringing, a stark contrast to the revolutionary milieu. But behind his spectacles, eyes sparkled with the same fervent idealism that painted the walls with whispers of "Swaraj". Savarkar welcomed Madanlal with a curt nod, the elder tigers recognising a kindred spirit in each other. Madanlal, drawn to the aura of power and conviction around Savarkar, felt a thrill of anticipation. He had devoured Savarkar's fiery essays, each word igniting a flame within him. Here, in this dimly lit room, he hoped to find not just guidance, but the fuel to turn his simmering discontent into a blazing inferno. As the night deepened, conversation flowed like the potent chai, punctuated by the clatter of spoons against bone china. Savarkar, his voice a deep baritone, spoke of the injustices inflicted upon India, his words weaving a tapestry of humiliation and exploitation. He spoke of the valiant martyrs who had challenged the Raj, their sacrifices a torch lighting the path to freedom. He spoke of armed resistance, of the bomb as a tool to awaken the world to the plight of his motherland. Madanlal listened, entranced. Each word resonated with the turmoil within him, the simmering anger at the sight of his fellow Indians treated as lesser beings in their own land. He recognized the truth in Savarkar's words, the echo of his own unspoken thoughts. The pamphlet, "The Cult of Bomb," no longer just words on paper, became a manifesto, a blueprint for action...

This night at India House wasn't just a meeting of two individuals; it was the turning point in Madanlal Dhingra's life. The seed of doubt, planted by Savarkar's words and fanned by the revolutionary fervour of the room, bloomed into a dark, unwavering resolve. Madanlal left India House not just a changed man, but a soldier in a silent war, forever etched in the memory of that smoky room where, beneath the London fog, a spark ignited a revolution.

Amritsar!!! The holy city pulsed with a frenzied rhythm. The air, thick with the scent of incense and sandalwood, carried the distant murmur of prayers and the rhythmic clang of temple bells. But beneath the veneer of piety, a storm was brewing. Whispers of rebellion danced on the wind, carried by the saffron dust that swirled through the narrow alleys. In this crucible of discontent, amidst the cries of vendors and the clatter of tongas, bloomed a rose of revolution - Madanlal Dhingra. His life, an intricate tapestry woven with threads of discontent and filial duty, played out against the backdrop of a nation straining for independence. From the vibrant chaos of Lahore's student protests to the stoic halls of London's academia, Madanlal sought the language of resistance. He devoured forbidden literature, each page a whispered manifesto, each word a sharpened shard of rebellion piercing his heart. Madanlal, the scholar disguised as a loyalist, carried the weight of two worlds on his slender shoulders. His father, a cog in the colonial machine, remained an ardent loyalist, oblivious to the fire gnawing at his son's soul. This internal conflict, a chasm wider than the ocean that separated them, added a poignant layer to the tragedy that unfurled. He had chosen his target with meticulous precision - William

Curzon Wyllie, the embodiment of colonial power, the architect of policies that strangled his motherland. In the echoing halls of Caxton Hall, a single gunshot shattered the oppressive silence, the echo ricocheting across continents, leaving behind a trail of shock and controversy. Madanlal, unrepentant and defiant, stood tall in the court, his words a scathing indictment of British rule. He embraced his fate with the quiet dignity of a martyr, his sacrifice a torch illuminating the path to freedom for a generation to come...

Madanlal Dhingra

A Young Life Bathed in Privilege and Discontent...

Born on 18th September 1883 in Amritsar, Madanlal Dhingra wasn't destined for rebellion. His family, wealthy and well-respected, belonged to the upper echelons of Indian society under British rule. His father, Dr Ditta Mal Dhingra, was a celebrated civil surgeon, a symbol of assimilation and loyalty to the Raj. Despite this comfortable reality, a storm brewed within young Madanlal. Up till 1900, Dhingra attended MB Intermediate College in Amritsar. After that, he travelled to Lahore to attend Government College University. The nascent nationalist movement, which at the time was focused on achieving Home Rule rather than independence, had an impact on him in this regard. Dhingra was particularly disturbed by India's poverty. He read a great deal about the causes of hunger and poverty in India and concluded that the Swadeshi movement and swaraj, or self-government, were the main places to look for answers. Here, he encountered whispers of dissent, his mind absorbing the revolutionary ideas swirling around him. He devoured forbidden literature, his spirit resonating with the writings of Mazzini and Garibaldi, fiery champions of freedom against tyranny. The streets of Lahore became his crucible, where he participated in student protests, his voice blending with others demanding an end to British rule. With special zeal, Dhingra supported the Swadeshi movement, which promoted Indian industry and entrepreneurship while opposing the import of British and other foreign goods in an effort to make India more self-sufficient. According to him, one of the main reasons India's economy hasn't developed is because the colonial government's industrial and financial policies were intended to discourage homegrown manufacturing and encourage the purchase of British goods.

As a Master of Arts student in 1904, Dhingra organised a student demonstration against the college blazer's British-imported fabric, which was ordered by the principal. For this, he was kicked out of college. The man's father, who was not fond of 'agitations' and held a lucrative job in government service, advised him to apologise to the college administration, refrain from engaging in similar activities in the future, and stop the expulsion. Dhingra declined and decided to take a job and live according to his own preferences rather than even returning home to talk with his father about the situation. As a result, Dhingra accepted a position as a clerk in a company that provided Tanga carriage services to bring British families to Shimla for the summer after being expelled from the area. He was employed as a factory worker after being fired for disobedience. In one instance, he attempted to form a union but was fired for it. After relocating, he spent some time working in low-paying jobs in Bombay. His elder brother, Dr Bihari Lal, forced him to go to Britain to finish his higher studies because by this point his family was really concerned about him. In 1906, Dhingra eventually gave his consent and left for Britain to study mechanical engineering at University College, London.

The India House and a Fateful Encounter...

Shyamji Krishna Varma, an intelligent scholar graduate of the Balliol College, Oxford, bought a home at 65 Cromwell Avenue in London in 1905 to serve as the dorm for students. On July 1, 1905, Henry Myers Hyndman, President of the Social Democratic Federation and supporter of India's independence, officially opened this as India House (The current India House, also known as the Indian High Commission, was constructed in the late 1920s and opened by King George V and Queen Mary on 8 July 1930. This India House should not be confused with that building). Attending the event were Dadabhai Naoroji, Lala Lajpat Rai, Madame Cama, Harry Quelch from the 'Justice' periodical, and Mr. Sweeny from the 'Positivist Review'. An editorial describing Shyamji's work in London, including his founding of the students' dormitory "India House", appeared in Lokmanya Tilak's "Kesari" in 1905. Savarkar studied Tilak's Kesari at Pune, where he read of Shyamji's efforts. Additionally, he happened upon a copy of Shyamji's monthly publication, "Indian Sociologist", which featured details on scholarships that Shyamji was providing to students in India. Savarkar submitted his scholarship application in March of 1906, which eventually paved the way for his further path to put a fight against the British across the borders. In addition to providing a reference, Tilak provided him the assurance that Savarkar had no plans to apply for any government jobs. Savarkar thus landed in London on June 15, 1906. Though Savarkar's stated purpose for travelling to London was to study law, he had other plans. In addition to noting the British people's shortcomings and considering strategies to use them to free India, he wished to personally witness the British people's strengths, which allowed them to govern the country. In addition, Savarkar aimed to recruit Indian students who were studying abroad for India's independence movement by establishing contact with them. Compared to India, these encounters were simpler in London. Approximately 700 Indian students were enrolled in British educational institutions in 1907, with 380 of them based in London. Additionally, Savarkar desired to connect with revolutionaries in other nations, including Egypt, Iran, Turkey, Russia, China, and Ireland. His goal was to become friends with them, learn how to make bombs from them and use both their friendship and their knowledge to try to topple British rule. Additionally, he desired to bring ammunition and handguns into India...

Savarkar's operations in London happened at an astonishingly fast pace. From 1906 until 1910, there was no shortage of news about India House. Savarkar organised weekly Sunday gatherings to talk about a range of future-related issues in India. It quickly gained popularity among students in India. Savarkar had given an interview to Campbell Green of the 'The Sunday Chronicle' in March 1909. His words reflected the right course of nature and the astonishingly increasing popularity of the India House. He stated, "India House is an inexpensive hostel. But for admission as a lodger, one does not need to have any specific political opinion. All that he has to do is to pay one pound (per week) for board and lodge. Political discussions do take place. Persons like yourselves and those who say that the British Raj is a 'divine dispensation' also come here. Discussions take place. Those who can convince others using truth and logic win the day".

The prominent, and prolific members of the India House were as follows - Bhai Parmananda, Lala Hardayal (founder of the "Ghadar Party"), Virendranath Chattopadhyaya (revolutionary and brother of Sarojini Naidu), Senapati Bapat, Hemachandra Das, MPT Acharya, VVS Aiyar, Gyan Chand Varma (secretary of "Abhinav Bharat"), Dadabhai Naoroji, Lala Lajpat Rai, Bipin Chandra Pal, Madame Cama, Sardar Singh Rana, Dadasaheb Karandikar and Khaparde (both of Tilak's lawyers), Ravi Shankar Shukla (later Chief Minister of Madhya Pradesh), Saiyyad Haider Raza, Asaf Ali, and Shapurjee Saklatwala (nephew of Dadabhai Naoroji and founder of the Communist Party of Britain). Remarkably, Savarkar was introduced to a young Barrister Mohandas Karamchand Gandhi in India House for the first time. The India House members used to be frequented by revolutionaries from Egypt, Ireland, Russia, China, and Turkey. Vladimir Lenin was one of these Russian revolutionary attendees!

India House Members (Credits: " Savarkar - Echoes From A Forgotten Past, 1883-1924 " by Dr. Vikram Sampath)

In 1906, Madanlal set sail for England, ostensibly to pursue engineering. However, beneath the academic veneer burned a deeper purpose - to understand the enemy from within. London, the heart of the British Empire, greeted him with a cold embrace. The imposing structures and bustling streets served as constant reminders of the power he sought to challenge. Yet, London also offered him sanctuary. He discovered India House, a haven for young Indian revolutionaries. Here, he met Veer Savarkar, Shyamji Krishna Verma, and other firebrands who stoked the flames of his revolutionary spirit. Their fiery speeches and writings echoed his discontent, providing him with a sense of belonging and purpose. Madanlal was tall, attractive, and well-built. He enjoyed having fun, so it was no surprise that he attracted attention from both young men and women. The buddies of Madanlal were gregarious and frequently sang romantic songs. For a short while, Madanlal became sidetracked and his sense of patriotism vanished from his consciousness. He had become accustomed to the 'warmth' of London through partying and infatuation with Caucasian women. Savarkar was passionately speaking about India's freedom during one of the Sunday sessions held at India House. In the next room, Madanlal and his pals were making a lot of noise. Savarkar was obliged to break off his speech to look into the adjoining room due to the din. He observed Madanlal and his pals having fun there. "What's wrong, Madan? You talk of gallantry and action, but you never show up to our weekly meetings??!". Savarkar chastised, "Is this the bravery you keep talking about?!" Dhingra was ashamed of the words. He departed India House without making eye contact with Savarkar for a few days. He had plucked up the guts to return to India House, mainly to see if Savarkar was still irritated with him. Savarkar acted as though nothing had happened between them when they first met. Remarkably, Dhingra was known to often come and practise at a shooting range on Tottenham Court Road after he moved away from India House. Additionally, he became a member of the "Abhinav Bharat Mandal", a Secret Society that was founded by Savarkar and his brother Ganesh Savarkar! Madanlal spoke in an equally loving manner. He questioned, "Has the time for martyrdom come?" with confidence. "If a martyr has decided and is prepared, it is generally accepted that the time for martyrdom has arrived!" Savarkar retorted. Savarkar, had thus, roused Dhingra's admiration in the 'cult of assassination', and now, Madanlal was ready to strike and deliver a Vajraghaat to the mighty British!

Target Locked..! and The Martyr is Ready!!...

It was now Madanlal Dhingra's decision, as he had made up his mind. In July 1908, he purposely joined the 'National Indian Association'. To dissuade Indian students from choosing a militant route, this Association was making a paramount effort. Their events were attended by prominent British dignitaries, and together with the 'proper' people (who were loyal to the British), Dhingra opposed (and supposedly denounced) Savarkar and other revolutionaries. The secretary of the "National Indian Association", Miss Emma Josephine Beck, quickly gained his trust. Through her, he learned the schedules of prominent English guests attending different events. The chance finally presented itself, and Dhingra seized it completely. Dhingra departed India House to demonstrate his disagreement with Savarkar after deciding on his mission. Following the Easter holiday in 1909, he moved in with Mrs. Harris at 108 Ledbury Road, London W11. A few weeks before Curzon Wyllie's murder, Dhingra attempted to assassinate Lord Curzon, the erstwhile Viceroy of India. In addition, he had also intended to kill Bampfylde Fuller, the previous lieutenant governor of East Bengal, but he was running late for a conference that the two were supposed to attend, thus he was unable to execute his plan. And now, Dhingra made up his mind to murder Curzon Wyllie. It is important to note that this was not another Englishman being killed because of his name similar to that of Lord Curzon. Curzon Wyllie held a high rank in the military. Curzon Wylie enlisted in the Indian Political Department in 1879 after first joining the British Army in 1866. He had distinguished himself in the 1879-1880 Afghan War, in Awadh, Nepal, Central India, and most importantly, in Rajputana, where he attained the highest rank in the Service. He was designated in 1901 to serve as the Secretary of State for India's Political Aide-de-Camp. Notably, he was also the chief of the Secret Police, something that is not reported in British publications nowadays. He had put an informant at India House in an attempt to obtain information about Savarkar and the revolutionaries. He went by the name "Kirtikar" and claimed to be a dental student. Savarkar discovered Kirtikar's true identity. Kirtikar handed Savarkar all the information he knew about the police operations after being exposed and facing death threats.

Curzon Wyllie had also played a monumental role in denying Savarkar the right to practise his law and sentencing his brother Ganesh (a.k.a. 'Babarao' Savarkar) to a life sentence in Andaman's cellular jail. This deed of Wyllie enraged the revolutionaries who were proactive in London and also culminated in his death, in the hands of none other than Madanlal Dhingra.

Savarkar became a member of the esteemed 'Grays Inn' on June 26, 1906. On May 5, 1909, following the completion of his studies, he was supposed to be called to the bar and begin practising law. Harnam Singh and Vinayak Damodar Savarkar both passed the final exam. However, Curzon Wyllie was attempting to prevent Harnam Singh and Savarkar from being called to the bar. Harnam Singh was therefore advised that there would be no more legal action taken against him, but that the Treasurer would chastise him in front of the Bench. Savarkar was scheduled to appear in court on three counts:

(1) That he incited the Nation of India to revolt by participating in seditious meetings and helping to distribute leaflets.

(2) The fact that he supported the killing

(3) That he said he was in favour of killing someone.

Ganesh Savarkar, Veer Savarkar's older brother, was given a life sentence of transportation on June 8, 1909. Pans and brooms were among his earthly belongings that were seized. Yesu, his wife, was left impoverished, homeless, and in need. For a while, she sought safety at the nearby crematorium. She died childless in 1918 and never saw her husband again. The only evidence the prosecution had was that he had published four allegedly seditious historically glorified poems. "Ganesh Damodar Savarkar convicted under section 121 and 124A of the India Penal Code and sentenced to transportation for life and forfeiture of property", was the message Viceroy Lord Minto conveyed to the Secretary of State for India three days later.

Meanwhile, Madanlal Dhingra was playing his cards well! With the help of the National Indian Association, he was able to gain the trust of many loyalists and direct servants of the Raj. Although he had publicly denounced all the members of the India House, he was doing multiple rendezvous with many prominent revolutionaries. Vinayak Damodar Savarkar was, of course, included in that list with whom Madanlal discussed his secret plans and sought inspiration. Now, on June 29, 1909, Dhingra had completed his arrangements. That evening, he went to Bipin Chandra Pal's house and met Savarkar. At the conference was Niranjan Pal, the son of Bipin Chandra Pal (who later became a director, screenwriter, and playwright in the silent and early talkie eras of Indian cinema). Dhingra appeared to be in a really positive mood. Savarkar and Dhingra exchanged warm words with one another. Savarkar told Dhingra what he was going to say when he killed Curzon Wylie. Savarkar asked Dhingra to commit the statement to memory after Niranjan Pal transcribed it. After giving Dhingra a Belgian-made Browning pistol, Savarkar invoked the highest of the spirits of Madanlal by taking a promise from him that he (Madanlal) would never show his face to Vinyaka if he now fails in his task! The two great friends, Madan and Vinayak departed with a lot of fondness and affection for each other in their hearts.

The D-Day, the Old Bailey and the Supreme Sacrifice...

It was July 1st, 1909. When Santiago, a Sinhala friend of Dhingra's, visited his home in the morning, he did not see any behavioural changes in Dhingra. It seemed like just another day for this fun-loving, jolly personality. But deep down inside, Madanlal was madly excited - An Excited David to end a Goliath's tyranny, An Excited Friend who was ready to make his friend proud, An Excited Indian who was about to fill tremors in the hearts of the British!!

Now, it was almost noon. At the Imperial Institute, where an annual function was hosted by an association called the 'Indian National Association' (not to be confused with the National Indian Association), Dhingra met a man named 'Koregaonkar' who was to follow him. Madanlal ate an early lunch and had afternoon tea at his own house, 108 Leadbury Street. At around 2:00 PM, he took off from his house with a pistol. He purchased a brand-new dagger and placed it in his pocket along with a leather sheath. He then proceeded to his training area, known as 'The Funland', and fired 12 shots at a range of eighteen feet. Eleven of these were absolute bull's eye! He was wearing a blue Punjabi turban and a lounge suit around 7 p.m. He slipped his loaded Colt pistol into his right coat pocket. He tucked one handgun inside his vest and another coat pocket. He couldn't remember the sentence (the statement that he was about to present after being arrested) that Savarkar had written, so he jotted it down in pencil on a piece of paper and stuffed it in his inner coat pocket with some cutouts from newspapers. He pocketed 10 or 12 shillings. He headed for the event, hailing the first cab to approach. Dhingra arrived at the Imperial Institute for the scheduled meeting at approximately 8 in the evening. By coincidence, he had forgotten the invitation pass, but, he was admitted after signing the visitors' register because he was already a 'trusted' Associate Member. Koregankar also showed up carrying a handgun. Curzon Wyllie seemed eager to get out of there after the meeting was ended. *"Aji jaao na! kya karte ho!!"* Koregaokar immediately exclaimed to Dhingra. Now, Dhingra went up to Curzon Wylie pretending to have a conversation with him. The two went out of the hall, opening the glass door. Dhingra lowered his voice as they approached the landing, as though he wished to talk about something private. Curzon Wylie nearly reached Dhingra. Dhingra saw his chance, took the Colt pistol out of his coat pocket on his right, and fired two shots at close range. It was 11:20 p.m. Two additional shots were fired by Dhingra as Curzon Wyllie stumbled. A Parsee physician named "Cawas Lalkaka" attempted to intervene, but Dhingra also opened fire on him. Dhingra tried to kill himself, but his attempt was unsuccessful, and he was now being held tightly by other people. At last, Dhingra wrestled with his captors, eventually fracturing one of their ribs in the process, but he was fixed firmly to the floor. His captors did not let out a breath of relief until they had taken away his pistol. Dhingra's glasses were also tossed away during the altercation but he eventually obtained them after finalizing his surrender to the police, who had now come over to arrest him. Upon feeling

Dhingra's pulse, the examining physician was shocked to discover that it was perfectly normal. *"Do you want us to inform any of your friends about your arrest?"* the police officer questioned Dhingra after he was arrested. In a witty reply with a menacing gaze, Dhingra said, *"There's no need. They'll read about my arrest in the papers tomorrow"*. The police were investigating whether any of Dhingra's pals could be implicated. He proved to be equal to them. Dhingra was brought to the police station on Walton Street.

Madanlal Dhingra's trial began on 23rd July 1909 in the Old Bailey (The Central Criminal Court of England and Wales), in which he only represented himself. Using comments made by an ex-Army officer during Wyllie's death inquiry, the British Press levelled several harsh accusations against Dhingra. This was conducted in front of Mr. C. Luxmoore Drew, the coroner (investigator), at Kensington Town Hall. Dhingra declined to participate in the activities. Captain Charles Rollerton, a former Army officer from Broadhurst Gardens in Hampstead, was present at the inquest. This witness speculated that Dhingra's semi-dazed and dreamy demeanour might have been caused by the Indian beverage known as 'Bhaang'. He continued by saying that if the natives were about to commit an act of this nature, they frequently consumed Bhaang before going ahead! When the coroner asked Miss Beck, the National Indian Association secretary, if she thought Dhingra was under the influence of drugs, she replied negatively. She stated that Dhingra appeared to be in good health and was very composed. Dhingra's landlady, Mrs Harris, added that she did not believe he ever consumed Bhaang or took any other drugs. The first medical professional to attend the scene of the assassination was Dr. John Buchnan of Vauxhall Bridge. The doctor said that Dhingra was completely composed. In the crowd, he appeared to be the most composed man. Psychiatrists also evaluated Dhingra to see whether he was psychologically sub-normal. Their tests came out negative as well. Thus, it proved to be a failed attempt by the British to prove Madanlal Dhingra's act was an act of mental fanaticism and now, it was a golden opportunity for Madanlal to publicly state that his doings were in the interest of national importance and the British should contain their malicious and heinous intentions towards the Indians & India. Thus, on these grounds, Dhingra clearly stated that his act was totally in favour of his patriotism towards his nation and not because of any influence or any personal interest. Dhingra also conveyed his sincere sorrow for Lalkaka's unintentional demise. He claimed he wouldn't have been killed, had he not gotten in the way. There was no reason for him to die. Mr Horace

Smith was the magistrate of the court, and before the pronouncement of his verdict, Madanlal had made a historical statement which ultimately was made to perish in the annals of the Indian history lessons. It is this statement that his dear friend Vinayak had helped him with. Madanlal Dhingra roared like a lion when he stated:

"I do not want to say anything in defence of myself, but simply to prove the justice of my deed. As for myself, no English law court has got any authority to arrest and detain me in prison, or pass sentence of death on me. That is the reason I did not have any counsel to defend me. And I maintain that if it is patriotic in an Englishman to fight against the Germans if they were to occupy this country, it is much more justifiable and patriotic in my case to fight against the English. I hold the English people responsible for the murder of 80 millions of Indian people in the last fifty years, and they are also responsible for taking away £100,000,000 every year from India to this country. I also hold them responsible for the hanging and deportation of my patriotic countrymen, who did just the same as the English people here are advising their countrymen to do. And the Englishman who goes out to India and gets, say, £100 a month, that simply means that he passes a sentence of death on a thousand of my poor countrymen because these thousand people could easily live on this £100, which the Englishman spends mostly on his frivolities and pleasures. Just as the Germans have no right to occupy this country, so the English people have no right to occupy India, and it is perfectly justifiable on our part to kill the Englishman who is polluting our sacred land. I am surprised at the terrible hypocrisy, the farce, and the mockery of the English people. They pose as the champions of oppressed humanity - the peoples of the Congo and the people of Russia - when there is terrible oppression and horrible atrocities committed in India; for example, the killing of two millions of people every year and the outraging of our women. In case this country is occupied by Germans, and the Englishman, not bearing to see the Germans walking with the insolence of conquerors in the streets of London, goes and kills one or two Germans, and that Englishman is held as a patriot by the people of this country, then certainly I am prepared to work for the emancipation of my Motherland. Whatever else I have to say is in the paper before the Court I make this statement, not because I wish to plead for mercy or anything of that kind. I wish that English people should sentence me to death, for in that case, the vengeance of my countrymen will be all the more keen. I put forward this statement to show the justice of my cause to the outside world, and especially to our sympathisers in America and Germany".

Madanlal Dhingra received an obvious death sentence. But as the court rendered his decision, Dhingra repeated, *"I am proud to have the honour of laying down my life for my country. But keep in mind that we will get our chance in the coming days"*...

Madanlal's act had sent shockwaves through both India and Britain. He was hailed as a hero by his compatriots. But for the British, he was a terrorist, a dangerous fanatic. His trial was swift and brutal, the courtroom a stage for a clash of ideologies. Madanlal, unrepentant and defiant, used the platform to deliver a scathing indictment of British rule. Curzon Wyllie was shot dead by Dhingra while his brother Bhajan Lal was studying law at Greys Inn in London. Bhajan Lal went to the public gathering four days after the incident to denounce Madan Lal. As a result, when Bhajan Lal paid him a visit to the Brixton jail, Madan Lal declined to see him. Except for Dr. Bihari Lal Dhingra, his brothers abandoned the Dhingra surname shortly after their brother was hanged. They took on the last name Lal as their surname because their initial names ended in that letter (Chaman Lal Dhingra became Chaman Lal, and so on). Savarkar said in a mellow tone, *"I have come to seek your darshan"* when he visited Dhingra. Upon meeting, they were both overwhelmed. Savarkar's chest was filled with immense pride and Dhingra had an amazing glare in his eyes that he was going to receive a grand welcome from his fellow Indian ancestors who had given their blood, sweat and lives for this grand nation.

17ᵗʰ August 1909... The Soldier finally rests...

Dawn bled into Pentonville Prison like a seeping wound. Its wan light cast long, skeletal shadows across the stark white walls of Cell 72, where Madanlal Dhingra sat, a statue carved from quiet resolve. The clock ticked with metronomic indifference, each beat a hammer blow against the stillness of his vigil. The morning routine, orchestrated with grim precision, felt distant, its sounds muffled by the cotton wool of his thoughts. Footsteps echoed in the corridor, the metallic clang of keys a grim counterpoint to the symphony of whispers playing in his mind. Each whispered a memory – Amritsar's sun-drenched streets, the fiery speeches at India House, the chilling echo of the gunshot, right in the face of Curzon Wyllie. In front of Deputy Governor Hales of Pentonville prison, London Metcalf's Deputy Under-Sheriff read Dhingra the execution warrant and asked him the standard questions. However, Dhingra disregarded their inquiries and composedly approached the noose. The officers escorting him were astounded by his bravery. Officer Pierpoint waited for Dhingra at the hangman's noose. Dhingra smiled at him and went up the stairs to the platform. He wrapped the noose around his neck. The wooden platform beneath was removed shortly after that. Dhingra's corpse fell eight feet to hang. His lifeless body was kept dangling for thirty minutes, as was customary. There was no sign of terror on his body when it was brought down. It is believed that Madan Lal Dhingra said the following last words before hanging:

"I believe that a nation held down by foreign bayonets is in a perpetual state of war. Since open battle is rendered impossible to a disarmed race, I attacked by surprise. Since guns were denied to me I drew forth my pistol and fired. Poor in wealth and intellect, a son like myself has nothing else to offer to the mother but his own blood. And so I have sacrificed the same on her altar. The only lesson required in India at present is to learn how to die, and the only way to teach it is by dying ourselves. My only prayer to God is that I may be re-born of the same mother and I may re-die in the same sacred cause till the cause is successful. Vande Mataram! "

During his final days, Dhingra expressed his desire for his books, clothes, and other possessions to be liquidated and the proceeds donated to the National Fund. However, the Metropolitan Police (of London) seized these. Chief Inspector McCarthy removed two trunks. Dhingra had granted Nitinsen Dwarakadas ownership of his personal items through a letter. However, on December 31, 1909, the Bow Street Magistrate's court heard the matter and decided that as Dhingra had left no will, the police were under no obligation to give over Dhingra's possessions to Nitinsen (London Times, January 1, 1910). Dhingra desired that his remains be burned and that his final rites be carried out in accordance with Hindu Dharma. A large number of Hindus petitioned Mr Herbert Gladstone, the Home Secretary, requesting that Dhingra's body be given to them since Brahmins were prepared to carry out the final rituals. This request was turned down! A man sentenced to the gallows had his final wish refused! His remains were placed in a casket and interred inside the prison's walls. The rose of rebellion, though plucked from its stem, had bloomed forever in the hearts of his countrymen, a potent symbol of the price one pays for freedom, and the unwavering spirit that defies even the darkest of shadows. The silence that swallowed Madanlal was not the end, but the beginning. It was the birth of a legend, the echo of a shot that would reverberate through the corridors of history, a rose blooming forever in defiance, in the heart of a free India!!!

Aftermath, and the Legacy...

Savarkar desired that Dhingra's ashes be dutifully gathered and distributed throughout India. Some Englishmen acknowledged and accordingly pleaded for Dhingra's exoneration because of his brave patriotism. Editor of "Review of Reviews", Mr W.T. Stead was one of them. Stead supported India's independence and was a big fan of Savarkar. He had invited Bipin Chandra Pal to give talks at his house about Indian civilization. Stead's idealism had cost him three months in prison. Stead argued that Dhingra's death sentence should be commuted to life imprisonment since he had murdered in a fit of insanity in a letter to The Observer dated July 25, 1909. A similar view was voiced by The Evening Post in London. As these views were being voiced, VVS Aiyar, Nitisen Dwarkadas, and JS Master (the editor of the Gujarati daily "Parsee", based in Mumbai) met with John Morley, the Secretary of State for India, and asked to be given Dhingra's corpse so that his last wishes could be fulfilled. However, Morley insisted that Dhingra would suffer the same fate as an assassin who was discovered and hanged. King Emperor Edward VII was outraged by Dhingra's bravery. He wrote to Morley on August 17, 1909, requesting that Indians be prohibited from entering England unless they had a good cause. He became enraged at such pupils, who learned treason while in England and urged others back home. But, a few of the Morley's Council members preferred life in prison over death for Dhingra. They were afraid that his martyrdom would inspire more acts of vengeance. A life sentence for Dhingra was also supported by a few Cabinet members.

"No Christian martyr ever faced his judges more fearlessly or with greater dignity", writes British poet and writer Wilfrid Scawen Blunt (entry dated July 24, 1909) in his memoirs. *"If India could produce five hundred men, as resolutely without fear, she would achieve her freedom"*. Medical testimony presented during the trial said that Dhingra did not exhibit any signs of weakness or an accelerated heartbeat upon being taken into custody. Ireland distributed and pinned up pamphlets labelled "Ireland Honours Dhingra" on the day of Dhingra's martyrdom. As luck would have it, Blunt turned 69 on the same day as Dhingra's martyrdom. Blunt said, *"They (the British) had honoured him (Blunt) by hanging Dhingra on his birthday"*. Blunt exclaimed, *"Because this day would be remembered as Martyrs' Day for several*

generations!" Interestingly, some Cabinet members did show respect for Dhingra's martyrdom. Winston Churchill later revealed this to Blunt. *"Again we sat up late"* Blunt writes in ("My Diaries", Vol. 2, p. 288, entry for October 03, 1909). This was one of the many famous things that Churchill uttered. Regarding Dhingra, he mentioned that there has been a lot of conversation about him in the Cabinet. Lloyd George had conveyed to him his utmost respect for Dhingra's nationalistic outlook, in which he concurred, *"Two millennia from now, we shall recall him with the heroes of Plutarch, Regulus, and Caractacus. Churchill praised Dhingra's final remarks, citing them as the best ever made in the service of nationalism"*.

Lala Hardayal stated, *"Dhingra, the immortal, has behaved at each stage of the trial like a hero of ancient times"*, in an article published in "Vande Mataram" on September 10, 1909. Although Dhingra is eternal and has dealt English Sovereignty in India the death blow, England believes she has exterminated him. On December 12, 1976, Madan Lal Dhingra's coffin was dug up in front of Natwar Singh, who was acting as India's high commissioner at the time. The coffin was also returned to India by air around the same time!

Ultimately, Madanlal Dhingra's legacy defies easy categorization. He is a figure who inspires admiration and condemnation, a martyr to some, a terrorist to others. His story compels us to examine the nuances of history, to ask ourselves hard questions about the ethics of resistance, and to acknowledge the emotional complexity of fighting for freedom. One thing is certain: Dhingra's actions had a profound impact on the course of Indian history. They sparked debates about violence and non-violence, fueled the fire of revolution, and left an indelible mark on the collective memory of the nation. He remains a figure who invites us to engage in critical dialogue, to understand the multifaceted nature of heroism and sacrifice, and to continue the ongoing conversation about the price of freedom. So, what is Madanlal Dhingra's legacy? It is a rose with thorns, a symbol of both defiance and tragedy, a reminder that the fight for freedom is rarely simple and that the heroes of history often carry the weight of immense moral ambiguity. It is a legacy that demands critical engagement, open minds, and a willingness to grapple with the uncomfortable truths that lie within...

CHAPTER SEVEN

RAMPRASAD BISMIL AND ASHFAQULLAH KHAN

Mid-July, 1925...

The oppressive summer heat hung heavy over Shahjahanpur, cloaking the mango grove in a thick layer of humidity. Crickets chirped their rhythmic song, the only sound breaking the hushed whispers of the ten figures gathered beneath the emerald canopy. Among them sat Ramprasad Bismil, his eyes burning with the intensity of a thousand suns, and Ashfaqullah Khan, his expression stoic yet resolute. Tonight, they weren't just friends, comrades, or revolutionaries; they were architects of a daring plan, one that would leave an indelible mark on the Indian Historical Landscape - the Kakori Train Action. Pandit Ramprasad Bismil, the fiery poet with a heart of steel, broke the silence. "Brothers", his voice, a low rumble, resonated with the weight of their shared dream, "we've spoken of defiance, of striking a blow at the heart of the Raj. Now, the time has come to turn words into action".

Murmurs of agreement rippled through the group. Chandrashekhar Azad, the young 19-year-old lion with a mane of defiance, leaned forward. "But Bismil bhai, attacking a train is no small feat. We need a good plan, flawless and swift". Bismil nodded, his eyes glinting with a dangerous glint. "Indeed, Azad. The target: the 8 Down Train, ferrying Raj's coffers from Shahjahanpur to Lucknow. The date: August 8th, a date etched in our memories". A collective gasp filled the air. This act, they knew, wouldn't be just a robbery, but a potent symbol of their unwavering resistance.

"But how do we stop a moving train?" Shachindra Bakshi, the meticulous planner, voiced the crucial question. "Rajendra Lahiri!!", Bismil announced, his gaze turning to the young man, "will be our eyes and ears on the train. He'll pull the emergency chain, bringing the beast to a halt". Lahiri, his face etched with determination, nodded curtly. "I understand my role, Bismil bhai. The train will stop". The conversation then turned to the heart of the plan – disarming the guards and securing the money. Ashfaqullah Khan, his voice calm yet firm, outlined the strategy. "We'll be ten, armed with the German-made Mauser pistols and unwavering resolve. We overpower the guards quickly, ensuring no harm comes to passengers. The money bags, symbols of Raj's greed, will be ours". Keshab Chakravarty, the quiet observer, interjected, "But what if things go wrong? We're outnumbered, and the British retaliation will be swift and brutal". The room fell silent, the weight of their potential sacrifice settling upon them. Bismil, unflinching, met their gazes. "We understand the risks, brothers. But freedom comes at a cost. Are we prepared to pay it?!"—a chorus of affirmations filled the air. "We are!" they declared, their voices resonating with unwavering determination.

The following days were a blur of meticulous planning...

They practised their moves under the cover of darkness, their every step a silent rehearsal for the grand act. They procured disguises, maps of the train layout, and even forged documents in case of capture. Each detail, however minute, was meticulously woven into the fabric of their plan. As the fateful day approached, the tension crackled in the air. Yet, amidst the fear and uncertainty, a camaraderie blossomed. They shared meals, songs of revolution, and stories of their dreams for a free India. They were not just comrades; they were a family, bound by a shared purpose and an unwavering belief in their cause. Finally, the day arrived. 9th August, 1925. The humid August air hung heavy with anticipation as they gathered one last time, their faces grim yet resolute. Bismil, his voice choked with emotion, addressed them, "Remember, brothers, we fight not for riches, but freedom. Let our actions speak louder than our words. Let Kakori be a spark that ignites the fire of revolution across our motherland!" With a final embrace and a silent prayer, they embarked on their mission, their footsteps fading into the darkness. The mango grove, witness to their whispered plans and unwavering courage, stood silent, waiting to see if their audacious dream would become a reality...

Countless are examples, where people from different races, religions, castes and backgrounds have come together to fight for a common cause, an idea, or a revolution and set a magnificent example of what we call today as 'secularism'. One such great example is the duo of Ramprasad Bismil and Ashfaqullah Khan! Pandit Ramprasad Bismil - A name that is seared in the muniments of modern Indian history with a golden engraving. A poet, a writer, a leader, and in a true sense, a freedom fighter. On the other hand, Ashfaqullah Khan, a Pathan by birth came from a very humble background. His love for Urdu poetry, his compassion for Maadr-E-Watan and his unshakable spirit of brotherhood were the qualities that made him a 'blood brother' of Bismil. Both of them hailed from the small town of Shahjahanpur of the United Provinces (modern-day Uttar Pradesh) and both had a fiery past before meeting one another, which forged a rock-solid mentality of a staunch revolutionary. This is a tale of these two juggernauts, who inspired the future generation of revolutionaries namely Bhagat Singh, Rajguru, Sukhdev, Jatin Das, Subhash Chandra Bose, Batukeshwar Dutt, and many more!

Asfaqullah Khan and Pandit Ramprasad Bismil

Pandit Ramprasad Bismil - A Poet, and A Brave Yoddha!...

Born in Shahjahanpur district of the United Provinces on June 11, 1897, Ramprasad Bismil was the son of Muralidhar and Moolmati Devi. His family was Brahmin by caste. At home, he studied Hindi with his father, and then with the consent of his father, a maulvi took him to learn Urdu. Due to their financial circumstances and familial conflicts, his ancestors had left the Bundelkhand region of the former Gwalior state. Bismil's father opposed the idea of sending his son to an English-medium school, even though he wanted him to pursue a higher education and find employment. In his memoirs, Bismil claims that his mother convinced his father to let him pursue his higher education in English. But anyway, he did learn the English language, because Apni Khabar ho ya na ho, Dushman ki poori jaankaari hona zaruri hai! (It's fine if we know a little less about us, but we should know every precise detail about our enemies)! Also, from a very young age, Ramprasad developed a deep interest in poetry, especially patriotic poetry which proved to be a fuel that kept him inspired despite facing all the brutal adversities that he faced in his later life from the British.

But before the legendary revolutionary emerged, there was a young boy nurtured by ideals found not in a sword, but in the pages of a book: 'Satyarth Prakash' (The Light of the Truth). It was this transformative text, coupled with the influence of the Arya Samaj, that lit the fire of rebellion within Bismil's heart, setting him on a path towards defying an empire. Bismil's early life in Shahjahanpur was steeped in traditions. His father, a pious Hindu, instilled in him the values of discipline and devotion. Yet, a restless spirit simmered beneath the surface. The injustices of British rule, witnessed firsthand, cast a dark shadow on his young mind. It was during this formative period that Bismil encountered Satyarth Prakash, a revolutionary treatise written by Swami Dayanand Saraswati, founder of the Arya Samaj. Published in 1875, Satyarth Prakash was a scathing critique of social evils plaguing Indian society. It advocated for social reform, women's education, and a return to true Vedic values. But it was its call for national self-reliance and resistance to foreign domination that resonated deeply with Bismil. In its pages, he found not just a critique of the present, but a vision for a future free from colonial shackles. The Arya Samaj, with its emphasis on self-reliance, social upliftment, and national rejuvenation, became the platform for Bismil to translate his newfound inspiration into action. Drawn by its ideals, he joined the organization at a young age. The Arya Samaj provided him with a community of like-minded individuals, where he could discuss his growing dissent and explore avenues for resistance. Beyond mere discussions, Bismil actively participated in Arya Samaj's activities. He organized youth gatherings, secretly distributed revolutionary pamphlets, and immersed himself in the movement's ideals. The Arya Samaj became his training ground, honing his organizational skills and nurturing his revolutionary spirit. Satyarth Prakash, however, wasn't just a political manifesto for Bismil; it was a literary inspiration as well. The book's powerful prose and passionate arguments ignited a love for writing within him. He adopted the pen name 'Bismil' (meaning "wounded, restless") and poured his yearning for freedom into verses that crackled with raw emotion and defiance.

The year was 1915, and a wave of shock rippled through Shahjahanpur. News of revolutionary leader Bhai Paramanand's death sentence in the (First) Lahore Conspiracy Case had reached the young Ramprasad Bismil, stirring a storm within him. This wasn't just a distant event; it was a personal blow, a spark that ignited the tinderbox of Bismil's growing discontent with British rule. Bismil, then an 18-year-old student, was already gravitating towards revolutionary ideals. The injustices of British rule were ever-present, gnawing at his sense of justice. He was finding his fiery solace in the Arya Samaj, but it was the death sentence of Paramanand, a scholar and comrade of Lala Hardayal, that truly awakened the revolution within him. Paramanand was more than just another name in the news. He was a symbol of resistance, a voice for freedom silenced by the iron fist of the British Raj. Bismil, already influenced by Paramanand's writings and ideals, felt a personal connection with Paramanand. The sentence fueled his anger and frustration, transforming it into a burning desire for action. It was at this critical juncture that Bismil found a beacon and guidance in his friend, Somdev, a Swami associated with the Arya Samaj. Somdev recognized the raw emotions churning within Bismil and became his anchor, channelling his grief and anger into constructive action. He encouraged Bismil to express his feelings through poetry, a talent Bismil already harnessed. Fueled by Paramanand's execution and guided by Somdev, Bismil penned the powerful poem Mera Janm (My Birth). This wasn't just an elegy; it was a declaration of war. The poem resonated with raw emotion, vowing to avenge Paramanand's death and fight for India's liberation. It showcased Bismil's transformation from a young, brooding poet to a budding revolutionary. Mera Janm wasn't just a solitary expression; it became a rallying cry for other young minds yearning for freedom. The poem circulated within the Arya Samaj circles, drawing others into the fold and cementing Bismil's growing reputation as a fearless voice of dissent. Somdev's role extended beyond encouraging Bismil's literary expression. He introduced him to revolutionary literature, including works by Lala Hardayal and Swami Vivekananda, further fueling Bismil's ideological fire. Somdev also connected him with like-minded individuals within the Arya Samaj, creating a community of support and fostering a shared vision of an independent India. Thus, Bismil's journey wasn't solely triggered by Paramanand's death sentence. It was a culmination of factors –

the injustices of British rule, the influence of the Arya Samaj, the emotional outlet provided by poetry, and the invaluable guidance of Somdev. These elements converged to create a potent force, propelling Bismil towards a life dedicated to revolutionary action.

The year 1917 proved to be a turning point in Ramprasad Bismil's life. Young Ramprasad Bismil, already ablaze with revolutionary fervour, stood at a crossroads. Leaving behind the familiar confines of Shahjahanpur, he embarked on a journey to Lucknow, the bustling nerve centre of Indian political activity. Little did he know, this move would mark a pivotal turning point in his life, shaping him into one of the most significant figures in India's freedom struggle. Guided by the unwavering mentorship of Somdev, Bismil took on a bold endeavour in Lucknow. Somdev took the pseudonym Babu Harivans Sahai, organised a few youths including Bismil, and published a Hindi translation of *"America Ki Swatantrata Ka Itihas"* (*The History of American Independence*). This seemingly innocuous act resonated far deeper than just words on paper. Published with Somdev's total consent, this book wasn't just a historical account; it was a veiled message of inspiration and resistance. America's successful fight against British rule served as a powerful allegory, igniting flames of hope and possibility within the hearts of young Indians seeking their own liberation. This audacious publication placed Bismil on the radar of both revolutionaries and authorities, marking his initiation into the intricate and dangerous world of political activism. Lucknow wasn't just a publishing hub; it was a melting pot of political ideologies. Here, Bismil encountered the vibrant Garam Dal (Radical Wing) of the Indian National Congress (INC). Led by fiery personalities like Lala Lajpat Rai, Lokmanya Bal Gangadhar Tilak, Bipin Chandra Pal and others, the Garam Dal advocated for more aggressive methods to achieve independence, contrasting with the moderate approach of the mainstream INC. Bismil, already disillusioned with the moderate INC's slow pace of change, found resonance with the Garam Dal's radical ideals. He actively participated in their meetings, imbibing their philosophy of armed resistance and direct action. This association exposed him to a wider network of revolutionaries, further solidifying his resolve to pursue a more militant (appropriate, in a true sense) path towards freedom. This formative phase in Lucknow wasn't without challenges. The publication of America Ki Swatantrata Ka Itihas drew the ire of the British authorities, forcing Bismil to operate underground. But he wasn't alone. The bond of brotherhood within the Garam Dal provided him with a much-needed support system, allowing him to remain steadfast and undeterred in his pursuit of freedom.

Bismil's time in Lucknow wasn't just about translating a book or joining a group; it was about reformation and transformation. He arrived as a passionate poet seeking liberation, and left as a hardened revolutionary, ready to dedicate his life to the cause of an independent India. The experiences he garnered - the publication of revolutionary literature, the embrace of radical ideologies, and the forging of enduring bonds with fellow freedom fighters - shaped him into a legend that he was about to become.

By the second half of 1917, the embers of revolutionary spirit within Ramprasad Bismil had blossomed into a burning desire for action. Leaving behind the relative anonymity of Lucknow, he returned to his hometown of Shahjahanpur, ready to translate his ideals into concrete steps towards dismantling the oppressive British Raj. This period witnessed the birth of Matrivedi (Altar of the Motherland), a revolutionary organization that marked a crucial turning point in Bismil's journey and ignited a spark of defiance that resonated far beyond his hometown. The name Matrivedi itself held profound significance. It wasn't just an organization; it was a symbol of devotion to the motherland, a call to arms to liberate her from the shackles of colonial rule. This concept of sacrificing for the motherland drew inspiration from ancient texts and historical figures who had fought for their land, their people and their Dharma. Bismil wasn't alone in his mission. Recognizing the need for collaboration and experience, Somdev made him reach out to Genda Lal Dixit, a school teacher from a town named 'Auraiya'. Dixit, known for his strong connections with local dacoits, brought valuable networks and knowledge of guerilla tactics to the table. This unlikely alliance between a young, idealistic poet and a seasoned operative with access to resources set the stage for Matrivedi's activities. Similar to Bismil, Dixit had founded Shivaji Samiti, an armed youth movement named after Chhatrapati Shivaji Maharaj. The two brought together young people from the United Provinces areas of Itawa, Mainpuri, Agra, and Shahjahanpur to fortify their respective organisations.

On January 28th, 1918, Bismil's voice of rebellion reached a crescendo. He published a pamphlet titled "*Deshvasiyon Ke Nam Sandesh*" (*A Message to my fellow Countrymen*), a passionate call to action addressed to his fellow Indians. This wasn't mere rhetoric; it was a document outlining the injustices of British rule, highlighting the need for armed resistance, and urging every individual to join the fight for freedom. Accompanying the pamphlet was a powerful poem penned by Bismil himself, titled Mainpuri Ki Pratigya (The Vow of Mainpuri). Written in fiery Urdu, the poem resonated with raw emotion and unwavering determination. Bismil declared his oath to "erase the name of slavery from the world", vowing to "make the world free at least once". The poem wasn't confined to paper; it was distributed hand-to-hand, recited in gatherings, and even etched on stones, ensuring its message reached hearts and minds alike. Thus, in 1918, looting was carried out three times to raise money for their revolutionary organisations. At the 1918 Delhi Congress, people were selling publications that the U.P. government had banned, so police scoured Mainpuri and the surrounding area for them. After the books were discovered by the police, Bismil fled with them. A police force arrived and gunfire broke out from both sides while he was preparing for yet another round of looting between Delhi and Agra. Swimming underwater, Bismil dove into the Yamuna. Both the police and his friends believed he had passed away during the encounter. Dixit, on the other hand, was detained in the Agra fort after being caught along with his other friends. He then ran away and lived in hiding in Delhi. An official criminal case was then crafted against them. It came to be known as the Mainpuri Conspiracy Case. On November 1, 1919, B. S. Chris, the Judiciary Magistrate of Mainpuri, proclaimed Dixit and Bismil absconders and announced the verdict against all those involved.

Matrivedi's activities, limited though they were, held immense historical significance. Bismil's astounding writings and audacious actions not only instilled fear in the British Raj but also ignited a sense of hope and defiance within the Indian population. They inspired others to join the fight for freedom, paving the way for more organized and impactful revolutionary movements. Bismil's journey with Matrivedi didn't take place in a vacuum. It was part of a wider historical context marked by growing discontent with British rule. The Non-Cooperation Movement was gaining momentum, led by M.K. Gandhi, while the First World War exposed the vulnerabilities of the British Empire. These conditions fueled the flames of Bismil's rebellion, providing a fertile ground for his message to resonate. Though short-lived, Matrivedi was a significant chapter in Bismil's journey and India's fight for freedom. It highlighted the importance of community, collaboration, and audacious action in the face of oppression.

The year 1919 dawned on a simmering India. The embers of discontent ignited by World War I and the Rowlatt Act had morphed into a raging fire, fueled by the Jallianwala Bagh massacre. This period, spanning 1919-1920, would see Bismil emerge as a master of the underground, his name whispered with fear and admiration across the land. During this time, he produced many of his famous writings. He also translated two works from Bengali *('Bolshevikon Ki Kartoot' and 'Yogik Sadhan')* and made up Catherine or Swadhinta Ki Devi based on an English book. Among these was a collection of poems titled Man Ki Lahar that he and others had written. Through his efforts, he was able to publish all of these volumes under the Sushilmala series of publications. Following the release of all the prisoners involved in the Manipuri conspiracy case in February 1920, Bismil went back to his native Shahjahanpur and made a deal with the local authorities of the British Raj to abstain from revolutionary activities. Ramprasad's statement was also recorded in colloquial language and presented to the court. But little did he know, he was about to meet a friend who was also of an equal fervour for his motherland and as compassionate towards poetry as he himself was. A friend, who was about to become a blood brother, despite being from a completely different background. A comrade, who also equally despised the hypocritical tyranny of the Raj! Little did Mother India know that her immortal spirit had united a band of fearless lions who were about to sacrifice their life in her divine service!

Ram and Khan - A Match Made for the Motherland!...

"To every man upon this earth death cometh soon or late,
And how can man die better than facing fearful odds,
For the ashes of his fathers, and the temples of his Gods"...

For the young Ashfaq, these lines from the poetry of Horatius were a constant source of inspiration. Yet, who was Ashfaqullah Khan? Ashfaqullah Khan's name is occasionally used to highlight the secular nature of the Indian revolutionary movement as well as the idea of communal unity and the anti-colonial campaign in general. But his journey also had a deep ideological and political dimension that has been overlooked often, as his letters, journal, and poetry demonstrate.

In the Shahjahanpur district of the United Provinces, Ashfaqullah Khan was born on October 22, 1900, into a prosperous Pathan landlord family (who hailed from the Khyber province of Afghanistan). His parents were Shafiqullah Khan and Mazharunissa. In the wake of Gendalal Dixit's Mainpuri conspiracy (1918), he was initiated into the revolutionary cause. At the time, Ashfaq was enrolled in Standard 7th. After reading Patriots of the World, a book that his teacher had gifted him the following year, he concluded that "only those who die for their country become immortal". Ashfaq later stated, "These young men would have been recognised as nation-builders if they had been born in a free country!" in defence of the revolutionary youth who were denounced as seditionists by the British authorities following the Mainpuri incident. After reading the poem Mainpuri ki Pratigya, he wrote in his diary, "This poem became the foundation of my love for the nation". Even though he was aware of and inspired by the sacrifices made by Bengali revolutionaries such as Kanailal Dutta and Khudiram Bose, Ashfaqullah was first exposed to revolutionary politics when a police raid took place at his school to apprehend Rajaram Bhartiya, a student involved in the Mainpuri case. It was then that the youthful Ashfaqullah began searching the United Provinces for revolutionary groups operating there. He asked Banwari Lal, a friend of his, to put him in touch with the one who had been declared an absconder in the Mainpuri conspiracy case, and the one who had created the beautiful Mainpuri ki Pratigya - Ramprasad Bismil!

Mid-1920...

The year was 1920, and the air in Shahjahanpur crackled with a palpable tension. The embers of discontent fanned by the Jallianwala Bagh massacre glowed dimly, waiting for a spark to ignite them. In this charged atmosphere, two young souls, Ramprasad Bismil and Ashfaqullah Khan, crossed paths, their destinies forever intertwined. Bismil, a passionate poet with a pen sharpened by revolutionary zeal, had already established himself as a local voice of dissent. Ashfaqullah, a student brimming with righteous anger, sought an outlet for his burgeoning desire to fight for freedom. Their paths converged at a gathering organized by the Arya Samaj, a reform movement advocating social justice and national rejuvenation. Their first encounter wasn't in a clandestine meeting or a hushed exchange; it was amidst the bustling crowds of a local carnival. Bismil, ever the observer, spotted Ashfaqullah, his eyes blazing with youthful idealism, as he watched an audacious street play depicting the atrocities of the British Raj. Drawn by this shared spark, Bismil introduced himself. Hesitantly at first, Ashfaqullah responded, captivated by the intensity of Bismil's gaze. As they walked, their conversation flowed like a river, each sentence carrying the weight of a shared dream. Bismil spoke of his verses that whispered of rebellion, each word carefully chosen to paint a picture of an independent India. Ashfaqullah, drawn by the passion in his voice, recounted his own experiences, the injustices he witnessed, and the yearning for freedom that gnawed at his soul.

"Do your words not yearn to become action?" Bismil asked, his gaze searching Ashfaqullah's eyes.

"They do", Ashfaqullah replied, his voice firm. "But how do we translate whispers into roars?"

"Together", Bismil declared, a smile lighting up his face.

That day marked the beginning of a bond that transcended mere ideology. They discovered a deeper kinship - a brotherhood forged in shared anger, unwavering courage, and love for their nation. They spent hours discussing revolutionary literature, including the ones penned by Mazzini, Garibaldi and Bismarck, their voices echoing in the quiet corners of Bismil's haveli. Their discussions weren't confined to theory. They explored the activities of other revolutionary groups and their successes, and failures and learned from each other's experiences. As they got to know one another and their talks progressed, Ashfaq and Bismil both abandoned their early prejudices about the "other" community and became exemplary members of the community. Following the riots, Bismil and Ashfaq participated in other marches and campaigns around the Shahjahanpur area. Bismil, along with Ashfaqullah Khan, even ran a campaign for the secular Swaraj Party during the municipal elections.

Ashfaq claimed that the separation of India based on religious identity was what had allowed the British to colonise the country since these divisions prevented any kind of national consciousness from growing. He believed that ignoring these distinctions would only result in the continuation of colonialism. Additionally, Ashfaq thought that religion had simply evolved into a weapon of divide and rule, with sectarian poison being propagated among the Indian population at the request of the British administration. Regarding the issue of religious practices and beliefs, Ashfaq supported keeping them inside the confines of the home. While he did not condemn religion as such, he did object to its use in politics. His final message to his fellow Indians was to put aside religious differences and band together to oppose British oppression. Ram and Khan now dreamt of a united front, a force strong enough to shake the foundations of the Raj. In these conversations, the seeds of the Hindustan Republican Association (H.R.A.) were sown, destined to become a symbol of armed resistance in the future.

The Bedrock of an Armed Revolution - Hindustan Republican Association (H.R.A.)

The soil for the HRA was fertile ground, nurtured by a growing tide of anti-colonial sentiment. The Jallianwala Bagh massacre in 1919, a stark display of British brutality, served as a catalyst. Young Indians, disillusioned by the moderate methods of the Indian National Congress, yearned for a more forceful response. This yearning found expression in the formation of numerous revolutionary groups across the country, each with their vision and methods.

Ramprasad Bismil was one of the numerous Shahjahanpur residents who attended the Congress session in Ahmedabad in 1921. He was seated on the dias alongside Ashfaqulla Khan and veteran legislator Prem Krishna Khanna. Along with Maulana Hasrat Mohani, Bismil actively participated in the Congress session and succeeded in getting the highly discussed Poorna Swaraj (Total Independence) plan approved at the Congress General Body meeting. Mohandas Karamchand Gandhi, who opposed this proposition, was rendered powerless in the face of the youths' overwhelming demand. After their return to Shahjahanpur, Bismil and Ashfaq organised the youth of the United Province to rebel against the government under the veil of the Non-Cooperation Movement. Bismil and Ashfaqullah weren't alone. Other revolutionary groups like the Banaras Group, led by Sachindra Sanyal and Jogesh Chandra Chatterjee, shared similar aspirations. The vehement words and poetry of Bismil had such an impact on the people of the United Provinces that they turned completely against the British Raj. He was becoming a staunch leader of the commoners, who believed that independence could NOT be achieved through non-violence and, 'Dharma Hinsa Tathaiva Cha' (Violence against Adharma, for protecting the Dharma is necessary).

In February 1922, British authorities in Chauri Chaura Lathi-Charged a few agitated farmers who were a part of the peaceful non-cooperation movement protest. Some of the farmers bled to death in the process. The policemen then had to face the wrath of the farmers and a brutal repercussion. 22 police officers were set on fire as the public attacked the Chauri Chaura police station. Without first contacting any Congress executive committee members, Gandhi called an instant end to the Non-Cooperation Movement, because violence was involved in this. In the 1922 Congress session in Gaya, Bismil and his group of young people protested

Gandhi with great vigour. Congress' then-president Chittranjan Das resigned after Gandhi repeatedly refused to reverse his decision. A new Swaraj Party led by Motilal Nehru and Chittranjan Das was created in January 1923 by the affluent party faction, while a revolutionary party led by Bismil was formed by the young group. With Lala Har Dayal's approval, Bismil now travelled to Allahabad, where he collaborated with Bengali revolutionary Dr Jadugopal Mukherjee and Sachindranath Sanyal to develop the party's constitution in 1923. The organization's fundamental name and goals were written down on a yellow paper, and later on October 3, 1924, at Cawnpore (today's Kanpur), a Constitutional Committee Meeting was held, with Sachindranath Sanyal serving as its chairman.

'Hindustan Republican Association (H.R.A.)' - This was chosen as the party's name during this conference. Following a protracted discussion with others, Bismil was appointed Chief of Arms Division and Shahjahanpur District Organiser. He was also given the additional duty of being the Provincial Organiser of the United Provinces (Awadh and Agra). Jogeshchandra Chatterjee, a senior member, was assigned the role of Coordinator, Anushilan Samiti, while Sachindranath Sanyal was overwhelmingly selected as the National Organiser. Sanyal and Chatterjee both left the United Provinces after attending the conference in Kanpur and travelled to Bengal to continue expanding the movement.

The HRA's manifesto, penned by Sanyal, outlined its vision and ideology. It declared the establishment of a "Federal Republic of the United States of Hindustan" as its ultimate goal, rejecting the British dominion and advocating for complete self-rule. The document emphasized armed struggle as the primary means to achieve this goal, drawing inspiration from international revolutionary movements like the Irish Republican Army. The manifesto also called for the 'socialist' goal of eliminating "all systems which make any kind of exploitation of man by man possible" and universal adult suffrage. Agra, Allahabad, Benares, Kanpur, Lucknow, Saharanpur, and Shahjahanpur were among the cities where the HRA opened branches. Additionally, they produced bombs in Calcutta at Deoghar in Jharkhand (formerly Bihar province), Dakshineswar, and Shovabazar.

The Daring Raid and A Night the Raj Trembled - The Kakori Train Action of 1925...

The humid August night of 1925 hung heavy over the sleepy town of Kakori. Little did the passengers aboard the Number 8 Down train, chugging towards Lucknow, know that they were about to become unwitting participants in a drama that would send shockwaves through the British Raj. This was no ordinary journey; it was a carefully orchestrated heist, a rebellion against an oppressive regime, and a night when the H.R.A. sent shivers down the spine of the highest of the British authorities. At the helm of this plan were, Ramprasad Bismil and Ashfaqullah Khan. Bismil, known for his meticulous planning and sharp intellect, whereas, Ashfaqullah Khan, known for his smart leadership skills and boldness, had meticulously choreographed the operation. They carefully studied the train's schedule, identified weak points, and recruited a team of trusted HRA members (a total of 10 now) – Rajendra Lahiri, Chandrashekhar Azad, Sachindra Bakshi, Keshab Chakravarty, Manmathnath Gupta, Mukundi Lal, Murari Lal Gupta and Banwari Lal - each bringing their unique dexterities to the table. Out of these 10, Chandrashekhar Azad and Manmathnath Gupta were the youngest but had a mountain-like character built within them. Azad was 19, and Gupta was 17 at the time of this audacious train action. Their objective?

1. To finance the HRA via funds levied from Indians by the British government,
2. To express a strong disapproval of the British government's heavy tax collection from Indians, and mainly,
3. To attract public awareness by fostering a favourable perception of the HRA among Indians.

The plan was first implemented on August 8, 1925, the designated day. When the train came to an end, Bismil, Ashfaq, and the others planned to catch the 8-down by walking up to the closest station. The 8-down from Shahjahanpur thundered by the station on its way to Lucknow just as they were drawing near to it. The young warriors could only watch helplessly as their scheme collapsed before it could ever be implemented. It was imperative to select a different strategy right away. The very following day, August 9, 1925, Bismil and his friends were about to do something that would make them indelible members of India's bravery. The revised strategy was extremely straightforward: make sure the revolutionaries board the 8-down train well in advance of their intended looting location of the Treasury. In light of this, Bismil and his group travelled by rail from Lucknow to one of the intermediate stops where the 8-down was supposed to arrive. They had arrived far in advance, so there was no room for error at this point. As soon as the train roared into the station, the group divided into two and entered separate compartments as previously arranged. The others boarded the third-class compartment, while Ashfaq, Lahiri, and Bakshi boarded the second-class compartment. After boarding, they dispersed to minimise suspicion. The 8-down was leaving the station, slowly slipping into the annals of history, while the light was slowly going out.

Now according to the plan, Rajendra Lahiri pulled the emergency brake as soon as the train passed Kakori station, bringing it to a grinding halt. As if to investigate the unexpected stop of the train, Bismil and the other members of the team stepped out of their compartment. The 10 courageous individuals got out on the track, pulled out their German-made Mauser handguns, and told the other passengers to stay inside the train and not get out. By then, darkness had descended, making it difficult for any of the other passengers to identify the person causing the train's delay. Regardless, gunfire was occasionally heard to guarantee cooperation and deter any passenger from attempting to obstruct the path. The iron safe with the money inside was pushed out and the guard was overcome. The safe was too hefty to be carried with them, and carrying it would have made their escape more difficult. In light of this eventuality, Bismil had made arrangements for the safe to be pried open using a hammer and chisel. Now, attempts were being made in that direction, but the process was laborious and sluggish. There wasn't much time left, so they had to unlock the safe right now or give up on the job altogether.

Ashfaq paused the iron safe weighing heavily in his palm from holding the sledgehammer just as they were about to bust it open. It was the distinct sound of a train coming. However, how did the British find out about the plot and mobilise troops so quickly? Was there one of them a traitor? It appeared as though all the revolutionaries would soon be shot down and engaged in a firefight. The train approached like an all-consuming avalanche, swallowing everything in its path, and for the valiant boys of Bharat Mata, time stopped still. The train's clickety-clackety sound seemed to announce their death sentence. They all turned to face their commander, Bismil. Do they make a final stand and battle to the death, or should they leave the scene? It was then that Bismil observed the adjacent parallel railway track where the 8-down had come to a stop. It was not the British police but the Punjab Mail train that was drawing near. He gave the order to the other revolutionaries to hide their weapons, and the Punjab Mail shot past the 8-down and vanished into the night. Bismil was safe, as was his squad! Ashfaq completed opening the safe in a few seconds, and the cash was gathered onto a large sheet. After doing their work, the revolutionaries vanished into the night. After arriving in Lukcnow in groups of two or three, the squad split up to find several hiding spots for the night. After Bismil and his comrades successfully executed their bold scheme, the onus was now on the British to respond to the rail hold-up at Kakori. Bismil and his associates were able to pilfer a total of eight thousand rupees from the treasury. The majority of the money was in pennies, which were the third-class compartment tickets that were collected from regular travellers! However, throughout the entire activity, a regrettable occurrence also occurred. Manmathnath Gupta accidentally shot Ahmad Ali, a passenger lawyer, killing him; nonetheless, this turned the matter into a manslaughter case. Ali had gone down to meet his wife in the women's section.

The Kakori Train Robbery wasn't a full-blown victory in the traditional sense. Yet, its impact transcended the immediate outcome. It dealt a symbolic blow to British authority, demonstrated the HRA's audacity, and ignited a spark of hope in the hearts of millions yearning for freedom. The image of young revolutionaries daring to challenge the empire captured the imagination of a nation, inspiring countless others to join the fight. Each HRA member played a crucial role in the Kakori operation. Bismil's leadership and strategic planning were fundamental. Ashfaqullah's courage and unwavering commitment inspired his comrades. Lahiri's quick thinking and disguise ensured the train's halt. Each individual contribution, like threads woven together, formed the tapestry of this audacious act.

The Aftermath, and the Supreme Sacrifices...

The reputation of the British police, secret service, and government was severely damaged by the Kakori event. The local media and common people erupted in celebration as soon as word spread, fully aware that the freedom fighters had played a part. The British knew this as well, but they were unwilling to admit it in public for fear of looking foolish. They used all of their resources - informers, secret police, and powerful leaders, to apprehend the offenders since they were in a difficult situation. Despite the tremendous impediments they faced, the Indian revolutionaries did their best, but Bismil and his group understood from the start what was ahead of them.

The month-long arrests began. Out of the individuals who participated in the train action, just ten were among the almost forty revolutionaries, who were detained in the initial phase of the crackdown. People who had nothing to do with the event were also apprehended. Some of them, nevertheless, were released. In September 1925, Manmathnath Gupta was taken from Benaras. Azad was nowhere to be seen and had vanished into thin air! The campaign suffered a worse setback on October 26, 1925, when Bismil was arrested from his hometown Shahjahanpur. The police also arrested Thakur Roshan Singh, who was not directly involved in the Kakori incident, on September 26, exactly one month ago. Rajendra Lahiri, who had travelled to Calcutta from Lucknow to join in bomb-making training, was taken into custody on January 10, 1926. Sachindranath Sanyal, the ardent mentor of revolutionaries at that time, was arrested (also from Calcutta) a month ago on 10th December 1925.

To first avoid being arrested, Ashfaqullah fled to Nepal. After that, he travelled to Kanpur, where he was introduced to Ganesh Shankar Vidyarthi, the renowned freedom fighter and purported editor of a newspaper called Pratap, before departing for Daltonganj, which is located in the Palamau region of Jharkhand. He worked there for six months as a clerk under a fictitious name. Ashfaq arrived in Delhi intending to leave India and carry on his revolutionary work from a place that would be safer. Here, he was approached by a friend in the market who pleaded with him to return home. Sadly, Ashfaq's "friend" turned out to be a British spy and on December 7, 1926, Ashfaq was taken into custody when his identity was revealed. The only people to avoid the British nets were Murari Sharma and Chandrashekhar Azad. The reason the British were unable to find Murari Sharma was that his true name was Murarilal Gupta. The riddle would remain unsolved until his son revealed this information later in 1997!

"Desh Ke Navratna Giraftaar!" (The nine jewels of the nation are arrested!) *- 'Pratap' (Kanpur), December 1926*

Now that all of the main conspirators had been taken into custody, the Kakori incident trial got underway. The case was being tried in Lucknow, where all of the freedom fighters were sent. The issue had garnered extensive media attention, and prominent firebrand leaders of that era, such as Lala Lajpat Rai, offered their backing. Gobind Ballabh Pant and Motilal Nehru assisted in setting up the funding and legal assistance. The

British were represented by lawyer Jagat Narain Mulla. Mulla's wife was Jawaharlal Nehru's relative, and Motilal Nehru had attempted to hire Mulla for Bismil and his pals. But Mulla agreed to argue on behalf of the crown when the British government made him a far more lucrative offer while he was considering the other proposal. Furthermore, Mulla personally held a grudge against Ramprasad Bismil since he had represented Bismil as a barrister in a previous case, and they had clashed on a few occasions. It was now the time to settle some old grievances. The barrister and family were to gain several lakhs of rupees in wealth during the duration of the litigation.

The British administration aimed to portray the revolutionaries as little more than petty thieves and dacoits. The jail amenities provided to them were inadequate and did not align with their classification as political prisoners. A few weeks after being imprisoned in Lucknow, Bismil and his associates began a hunger strike. They want to be treated like political prisoners, with better food, access to books and newspapers, a pen and paper for writing, and the ability to have visits under strict guidelines. To end the hunger strike, the prison administration began force-feeding the revolutionaries and cracked down on their activities. The jailers' attempts to put a stop to the hunger strike were all unsuccessful. This was the first time in the history of the Indian independence movement that a sizable group of inmates had joined forces to embark on a hunger strike to demand what they wanted. After sixteen days, the government gave in and promised to provide them with better food and to treat them like political prisoners. Even if the triumph was tiny, it established the precedent for similar instances from the jail in Lahore, where Bhagat Singh was held, to the jail in Cellular, where Veer Savarkar and several others were held. The Kakori trial proceeded unabated throughout this time. The British authorities made every effort to fabricate proof that would link the revolutionaries to the crimes. One of the people involved in the train hold-up, Banwari Lal, changed his role to approver. At last, the British had a solid case against Bismil and his associates. There were also shades of an 'Escape Plan' running through the brains of these revolutionaries. But the newly turned approver, Banwari Lal warned the authorities of these threats and the British tightened the security and constricted every moment of any revolutionary, inside or outside of their custody. Another plan called for smuggling a hypnotic substance called 'chloral' into the prison, mixing it with the food, and giving it to the jail guards. The idea was that the revolutionaries would escape when the guards fell asleep. Although this was attempted with great zeal, it was discovered that the chloral that was given to them was tainted and ineffectual. As each escape strategy fell apart, the revolutionaries realised their time for reckoning had come.

On April 6, 1927, the day of judgment was set. The British dubbed it King Emperor versus Ramprasad and others, using a supposedly exquisite language. The jail observed Qatl Ki Raat, or "the night of the murder" the night before the verdict. The decision was given out by Judge Hamilton the next day, on April 7, 1927. The prominent sections of that judgement were as follows: Rajen Lahiri, Thakur Roshan Singh, and Ramprasad Bismil were all given the death penalty. Transportation to the Andaman and Nicobar Islands' Cellular Jail for life was imposed on Sachindranath Sanyal. Sachindra Bakshi and Manmathnath Gupta will serve 14 years in prison. Banwari Lal received a 2-year sentence, and Mukundi Lal received a 5-year sentence. Following the announcement of the decision, all of the inmates were marched off to separate cells in the Lucknow jail after having their collective portraits taken. All of the revolutionaries were divided up and sent to various prisons in a matter of days. Lahiri was transferred to a jail in Gonda, Bismil was transferred to a jail in Gorakhpur, and Roshan Singh was sent to a jail in Allahabad. The funny part is that Judge Hamilton promptly left the courtroom to travel to London right after declaring the verdict. Retaliation for the sentences he gave down from other revolutionaries was what worried him the most!

After a separate trial, Ashfaqullah Khan received the same punishment: death by hanging. He was taken to the prison at Faizabad. With Ashfaq in particular, the British attempted their tried-and-true strategy of divide and rule with the revolutionaries. Ashfaq received a message from a British agent asking "how he could be so stupid as to associate with Hindu revolutionaries who desired to establish a Hindu government". "I don't think this is a Hindu conspiracy, and if it were, I would prefer the Hindu regime over the British regime", was Ashfaqullah Khan's firm reply.

Nationwide demonstrations were held in opposition to the court's ruling. The Viceroy of India was even petitioned by members of the Central Legislature to reduce the men's death sentences to life in prison. There were also Privy Council appeals. The Chief Court upheld the initial ruling on August 11, 1927, save for a single seven-year sentence from the ruling on April 6. The members of the legislative council timely submitted a mercy appeal to the U.P. provincial governor, but it was denied. On September 9, 1927, Ramprasad Bismil wrote a letter from Gorakhpur Jail to Madan

Mohan Malaviya. With the signatures of 78 members of the Central Legislature, Malviya addressed a memorandum to Irwin, the then-viceroy and governor-general of India, but it was also rejected. Through renowned English lawyer Henry S.L.Polak, the King-Emperor received the final mercy appeal on September 16, 1927, from the Privy Council in London. However, the British Government had already decided to hang the four prisoners, and they sent their decision to the Viceroy's office in India, stating unequivocally that they would all be hanged until death by December 19, 1927. The Pratap newspaper published by Vidyarthi featured several articles urging readers to resist this injustice. Regretfully, all of the pleas were ignored, and the British carried out the penalties - Ramprasad Bismil (30 years of age) and Ashfaqullah Khan (27 years of age) entered the gates of heaven on 19th December 1927, in the Gorakhpur Jail and Faizabad Jail, respectively. Thakur Roshan Singh made his supreme sacrifice on the same date, 19th December 1927 in Allahabad Jail, whereas, Rajendra Lahiri laid down his life for the nation on 17th December 1927 in the Gonda Jail...

An Enduring Legacy...

Both Bismil and Ashfaqullah embraced martyrdom for their cause. Their executions, along with those of their comrades, sent shockwaves through the nation, transforming them into potent symbols of sacrifice. Their unwavering commitment even in the face of death served as a powerful reminder of the price of freedom and the determination of the revolutionaries. Their martyrdom fueled the fire of resistance, inspiring countless others to take up the mantle of freedom. The impact of Bismil and Ashfaqullah transcended geographical boundaries. Their story resonated with anti-colonial movements across the globe, inspiring fighters for freedom in other countries. Their audacious acts and persistent commitment served as a rallying cry for those struggling against oppression, demonstrating that the fight for freedom was a universal one. It's important to remember that Bismil and Ashfaqullah weren't one-dimensional heroes. Their story is woven with the complexities of the historical context and the limitations of their time. However, these complexities shouldn't diminish the significance of their contribution and the ideals they represented. The grand legacy of Bismil and Ashfaqullah lies not just in their actions but in the ideals they embodied - courage, sacrifice, and an unwavering commitment to freedom. Their story serves as a reminder that the fight for justice is an ongoing pursuit, and their voices continue to inspire generations to speak out against oppression and strive for a better future. They left behind not just a legend, but a call to action, urging us to carry the torch of freedom forward, ensuring that their sacrifices were not made in vain. Their story encourages us to engage with the past critically, remembering both the triumphs and the complexities, and to learn from their experiences as we strive to build a more just and equitable world for us.

The tradition of the Kakori martyrs was now to be continued by a great number of brave warriors, such as Rajguru, Sukhdev, Bhagat Singh, and Batukeshwar Dutt. And still going free outside was the mighty 20-year-old Chandrashekhar Azad, the mentor of Bhagat Singh and the new ringleader of the Indian revolutionary toil!

CHAPTER EIGHT

CHANDRASHEKHAR AZAD

Ab bhi jiska khoon na khaula khoon nahi wo pani hai,

Jo desh ke kaam na aaye woh bekar jawani hai!

'If yet your blood does not rage, then it is water that flows in your veins. What is the flush of youth if it is not of service to the motherland?!'

Chandrashekhar Azad! A name that resembles unyielding determination, persistent courage, and profound love for the motherland. A name that used to give nightmares to the British Indian Police authorities and send shivers down the spine of the 'royals' and the 'loyals' of the British Empire. Chandrashekhar Azad wasn't just a name whispered with reverence in Indian history; he was a whirlwind of emotions, a man whose personality was as multifaceted as the fight for freedom itself. At the core of Chandrashekhar Azad's personality lay an unshakeable devotion to India's freedom struggle. From a young age, he was deeply moved by the injustices inflicted upon his fellow countrymen by the British Raj. This ignited a fiery passion within him, driving him to dedicate his life to the cause of liberation. Under the guidance of Ramprasad Bismil, Azad blossomed into a fearless and dedicated revolutionary. He strengthened his faith in the power of armed struggle to overthrow British rule. Azad's commitment to the cause was relentless, and he soon emerged as one of the most prominent leaders of the revolutionary movement. Azad's patriotism was not merely a sentiment but a guiding principle that informed every aspect of his being. Azad was characterized by his uncompromising determination to achieve his goals, no matter the obstacles in his path. He firmly believed in the power of armed struggle to overthrow British rule and never hesitated in his commitment to the cause. Despite facing immense pressure and constant surveillance from British authorities, Azad remained persistent in his pursuit of freedom. His fearless determination inspired those around him and earned him the admiration of fellow revolutionaries. Azad possessed a magnetic charisma that drew people to him and inspired them to join the struggle for independence. His tenacious commitment to the cause, coupled with his fearless demeanour, made him a natural leader among his peers. Azad's ability to rally support and mobilize resources was instrumental in galvanizing the revolutionary movement against British rule. He led by example, inspiring others to emulate his courage and dedication. To understand Azad is to delve into the burning passion that fueled his revolutionary spirit, the unwavering dedication that made him a leader, and the quiet compassion that resided beneath the surface...

Chandrashekhar Azad

Early life and the 'Azad' in the making...

The year is 1906. The British Raj casts a long shadow over India, a simmering discontent brewing beneath the surface. In the quaint village of Bhabra, nestled amidst the verdant Madhya Pradesh countryside, the Tiwari family welcomed a baby boy on 23rd July. Sitaram Tiwari and Jagrani Devi named the boy Chandrashekhar. His ancestors came from a village named 'Badarka' in the Unnao district of Uttar Pradesh.

Chandrashekhar's early life was steeped in a traditional Brahmin household. His father, Sitaram Tiwari, was a pious man, and his mother, Jagrani Devi, was a pillar of strength. Imagine young Chandrashekhar, his days filled with the gentle murmur of Sanskrit chants and the comforting aroma of spices wafting from the kitchen. There was a spark of defiance even in his early years, and it was the inherent yearning for freedom that resonated within him, a quality that would later define his life. Fate, however, had other plans. The family's idyllic existence in Bhabra was disrupted when they moved to the princely state of Alirajpur. This wasn't a mere change in scenery; it was a subtle shift that would unknowingly sow the seeds of rebellion in Chandrashekhar's young mind. Alirajpur, though seemingly untouched by the turmoil of British rule, was a microcosm of the larger discontent simmering across India. The murmurs of resentment against the British, carried on the wind by traders and travellers, reached young Chandrashekhar's ears. There, he witnessed firsthand the disparity between the opulent lifestyle of the Maharaja and the hardships faced by the ordinary people. These experiences, subtle yet impactful, undoubtedly played a role in shaping his nascent political awareness.

Chandrashekhar's thirst for knowledge was evident from a young age. His early education took place in a local gurukul, where he would have received a grounding in traditional Hindu scriptures and Sanskrit. His mother, Jagrani Devi, dreamt of her son becoming a great scholar. She envisioned him traversing the hallowed halls of Kashi Vidyapeeth, the renowned centre of learning in Banaras (now Varanasi). Imagine the excitement bubbling within young Chandrashekhar at the prospect of embarking on this intellectual journey. However, destiny had a different path in store. The bustling city of Kashi was a melting pot of ideas and ideologies, and it did not fail to expose Chandrashekhar to a new world. This vibrant intellectual hub was also a hotbed of political activity. Around that time, the Non-Cooperation Movement, spearheaded by Gandhi, was gaining momentum across India. Young Chandrashekhar's mind buzzed with fiery speeches and passionate discussions about freedom. The yearning for justice, already simmering within him found validation in these revolutionary ideas. In mid-1921, 15-year-old Chandrashekhar began to participate in the non-cooperation movements' protests, his spirit ignited by the collective call for the freedom of Bharat. One day, an incident turned out to be a turning point in his life and it made him transform - from a zealous teenager to a strong & stoic man. It made him tough and gave him the eternal strength he needed to have within himself to fight an upcoming battle that would make him a legendary revolutionary.

On December 20th, 1921, Chandrashekhar was detained for his involvement in the non-cooperation movements' demonstrations. He identified himself as "Azad" (The Free), his father as "Swatantrata" (Independence), and his domicile as "Jail" when he was brought before Parsi district magistrate Justice M. P. Khareghat a week later. The enraged magistrate gave him 15 lashings as punishment! Chandrashekhar now became very popular amongst the locals who now have started calling him Azad. His new identity made him an 'independent' person already and that's exactly what boosted the morale of Chandrashekhar. After this incident, he started forging himself physically, mentally & emotionally. One thing was absolutely clear in his mind - If yet your blood does not rage, then it is water that flows in your veins. What is the flush of youth if it is not of service to the motherland?!...

Chandrashekhar's early life, though seemingly ordinary, laid the foundation for the extraordinary journey that lay ahead. The values instilled by his family, the exposure to political realities, and the disillusionment with peaceful resistance – all these factors played a crucial role in shaping his revolutionary spirit. His journey from a young boy yearning for knowledge to a young man yearning for freedom wasn't a sudden transformation. It was a gradual awakening, fueled by experiences and observations. Imagine him leaving Kashi Vidyapeeth, a sense of defiance burning in his eyes. The expulsion, though a setback, might have felt liberating in a way. It freed him from the confines of traditional education, allowing him to pursue a more radical path.

Azad becomes a 'Krantikari'...

The year 1922 turned out to be a watershed in the life of 16-year-old Azad!...

4th February 1922 - At a place called Chauri Chaura (Gorakhpur district of the United Provinces), the police opened fire on a sizable gathering of protestors who were taking part in the Non-Cooperation movement. All the people inside a police station were killed when the protestors assaulted and set it on fire as payback. 23 police officers and three civilians lost their lives as a result of the event. Gandhi, who was adamantly opposed to violence, used this episode as justification to put an end to the National Non-Cooperation Movement on February 12, 1922. A biting chill hangs in the air, mirroring the sense of disillusionment that has gripped 16-year-old Chandrashekhar Azad. News of Gandhi's sudden suspension of the Non-Cooperation Movement, a mere eight days after the Chauri Chaura incident, sent shockwaves through the nation. For Azad, a young man brimming with hope for a free India, this news feels like a personal betrayal, a crushing blow to the spirit of rebellion that had begun to blaze within him. The Non-Cooperation Movement, a beacon of hope that had ignited a sense of collective power in millions of Indians, lay in ruins. Chandrashekhar's world had turned upside down. He had poured his heart and soul into the movement, participating in boycotts, strikes, and peaceful protests. The collective energy, the sense of purpose, and the belief that they were making a difference must have been intoxicating. Now, all that remained was a bitter taste of defeat, a sense of helplessness in the face of British brutality. Questions gnawed at Chandrashekhar's young mind: Was non-violence truly the answer? Could freedom be achieved through peaceful protests alone? The Chauri Chaura incident, though horrific, was a single act of violence against a system that had perpetrated countless atrocities on the Indian people. Was Gandhi's response an overreaction? Or was it a necessary step to prevent further bloodshed? Chandrashekhar Azad, like many young revolutionaries, saw this incident as a symptom of a larger issue. The British Raj wouldn't relinquish its power willingly. Their response to peaceful protests had been swift and brutal – the Jallianwala Bagh massacre was a stark reminder of that. Azad saw Gandhi's decision as a surrender, a retreat in the face of adversity. This clash of ideals – non-violence vs. armed resistance – brewed a storm within him. The suspension of the Non-Cooperation Movement wasn't just a strategic retreat; it was a symbolic defeat. It shattered the sense of unity and purpose that had galvanized the nation. Azad, witnessing the movement crumble around him, felt a deep sense of disillusionment. Did the path to freedom truly lie in peaceful protests, especially when faced with an oppressive regime?

For Azad, this disillusionment became the catalyst for seeking alternatives. He began to gravitate towards more radical elements within the Indian independence movement. The idea of armed resistance, once a fringe concept, has started to seem more appealing. Around the same time, he had heard of a secret organization called the 'Hindustan Republican Association (H.R.A)', and now, it all seems justified. Azad was now clear of his conscience about his destined path and he also took an interest day after day, minute after minute in taking an interest in all those activities that the HRA was involved in! And then, one fine day, he met someone who would introduce Azad to a new 'solace' of like-minded people who were also equally distressed over the spiritless decision of calling off the Non-Cooperation movement.

A young man named Manmathnath Gupta strides into Chandrashekhar's life. Gupta, a firebrand revolutionary himself, recognizes the simmering discontent within Chandrashekhar Azad. He becomes the spark that ignites the dry tinder of Azad's disillusionment. They used to engage in intense discussions, Gupta outlining the philosophy of the Hindustan Republican Association (HRA), a revolutionary outfit dedicated to armed resistance. The concept, once distant, now resonates deeply with Azad's burning desire for freedom. Gupta doesn't just introduce an ideology; he introduces a mentor – Ramprasad Bismil! Bismil, a charismatic leader and a founding member of the HRA, sees the potential in Chandrashekhar Azad. In their first meeting only, there occurred an exchange of fiery glances and a silent understanding forged in the shared yearning for a free India.

Chandrashekhar Azad's decision to join the HRA wasn't a mere formality. It was a conscious choice, a commitment to a more radical path. The disillusionment with non-violent methods paved the way for this ideological shift. Becoming a member of the HRA wasn't just about taking up arms; it was about joining a brotherhood of revolutionaries bound by a shared purpose. Chandrashekhar Azad's transformation wasn't an overnight metamorphosis. It was a gradual process fueled by experiences, discussions, and a deep-seated longing for freedom. His initial role within the HRA likely involved attending clandestine meetings, familiarizing himself with revolutionary ideals, and honing his skills in weapon handling. However, a talent for organization and a quick mind soon became evident. Also, the HRA, like any revolutionary outfit, needed funds to operate. This is where Azad's resourcefulness came into play. He devised strategies to raise money - which included planning daring robberies or forging alliances with sympathetic businessmen. Chandrashekhar's transformation wasn't just ideological; it was personal. His life now revolved around the cause of freedom. He likely shed the innocence of youth, adopting the cloak of a revolutionary. The comforts of home and family would have taken a backseat to the constant struggle for survival and the ever-present threat of capture, and a new journey, thus, had begun...

A daring act, and a narrow (smart) escape...

The Kakori Train Action of 9th August 1925 stands as a pivotal moment in India's struggle for independence, and at the tender age of 19, Azad played a crucial role in implementing the daring robbery that shook the foundations of British colonial rule in India. As a prominent member of the Hindustan Republican Association (HRA), Chandrashekhar Azad was also deeply involved in the planning and execution of the Kakori Train Action. Alongside his comrades, including Ram Prasad Bismil, Ashfaqullah Khan, and Rajendra Lahiri, Azad meticulously planned every aspect of the operation intending to strike a blow against British imperialism. On the fateful day of 9th August 1925, a group of ten revolutionaries, including Chandrashekhar Azad, boarded the 8 Down train from Shahjahanpur to Lucknow. Their target was the train's treasury carriage, which contained government funds (Taxes paid by the Indians) meant for financing British colonial activities in India. As the train chugged along its route, the revolutionaries sprang into action, overpowering the guards and seizing control of the treasury carriage. With precision and determination, they looted the funds intended for the British Raj, sending shockwaves through the colonial establishment.

Chandrashekhar Azad's role in the Kakori Train Action was multifaceted. As one of the key organizers and strategists of the operation, Azad provided crucial guidance and leadership to his comrades. His fearlessness and unwavering commitment to the cause inspired confidence in the other revolutionaries, driving them to execute the mission with precision and determination. Amid the chaos and excitement of the robbery, Azad remained calm and composed, directing the actions of his fellow revolutionaries and ensuring that the operation proceeded according to plan. His quick thinking and strategic acumen were instrumental in overcoming the obstacles posed by the train's security personnel and carrying out the robbery successfully.

However, the aftermath of the Kakori Train Action posed a new challenge for Chandrashekhar Azad and his comrades. With the British authorities launching a massive manhunt to apprehend the perpetrators of the robbery, Azad knew that his life was in grave danger. In a daring display of cunning and resourcefulness, Azad managed to evade capture while his fellow revolutionaries were arrested one by one. He employed a series of clever disguises and aliases to evade detection, moving from one safe house to another under the cover of darkness. Azad's ability to outsmart the British police authorities was a testament to his ingenuity and resolve. Despite the immense pressure and constant threat of capture, he remained steadfast in his determination to continue the fight for India's independence. Eventually, Azad, Keshab Chakravarthy, and Murari Sharma managed to escape being apprehended by the police. Chandrashekhar Azad's escape from the clutches of the British was a major setback for the authorities. It not only cemented his reputation as a skilled revolutionary but also served as a potent symbol of defiance. The Kakori Train Action, though a daring act, wasn't a complete military victory for the HRA. However, it achieved something far more significant – it instilled fear in the hearts of the British and ignited a spark of hope in the minds of millions of Indians yearning for freedom.

Eventually, the prominent members of the Hindustan Republican Association - Ramprasad Bismil, Ashfaqullah Khan, Thakur Roshan Singh and Rajendra Lahiri were hanged and many others were put behind bars. For the second time in his life, Azad felt like his dream of liberating his motherland was going to end abruptly and everything seemed jittery for him. But again, whatever happens, happens for a reason and now, Chandrashekhar Azad knew the ergonomics of leading an armed revolution and therefore, he needed to resurrect, rebuild & reorganise the ideals of the HRA. He needed funds and a good network of people, and both of these things were going to be the eventual fruits of time. Chandrashekhar Azad had profoundly realised that he needed to be patient instead of being restless. So, to buy out some time and get things in order once again, he changed his location on a quicker basis and thus, he now moved to a new town - Jhansi!

Azad in Jhansi - A Tale of Redemption and Resistance...

After narrowly escaping the clutches of the British police following the crackdown on the Hindustan Republican Association (HRA) members involved in the Kakori Train Robbery, Chandrashekhar Azad found refuge in the historic city of Jhansi. Here, in the heart of India's struggle for independence, Azad embarked on a new chapter of resistance and defiance against British colonial rule. His activities in Jhansi would not only solidify his reputation as a fearless revolutionary but also leave an indelible mark on the annals of India's fight for freedom.

Nestled on the banks of the Betwa River, Jhansi had long been a stronghold of anti-colonial sentiment, making it an ideal refuge for Azad and his fellow revolutionaries. Upon his arrival in Jhansi, Azad wasted no time in reaching out to like-minded individuals and organizations sympathetic to the cause of independence. He forged alliances with local leaders and activists, leveraging their support to further his mission of challenging British hegemony in India. Azad's charisma and determination won him the respect and admiration of his newfound allies, cementing his position as a central figure in the city's burgeoning independence movement.

Well-versed in marksmanship, he educated other members of his group in the art of shooting and utilised the 15-kilometre-distant forest of Orchha for practice. He constructed a hut next to a Hanuman temple on the banks of the Satar River, where he spent a considerable amount of time living under the pseudonym "Pandit Harishankar Bramhachari". By working as a teacher for kids from the next hamlet of Dhimarpura, he was able to build strong relationships with the locals. Azad also set about organizing clandestine meetings and gatherings aimed at mobilizing the local populace against British rule. He delivered impassioned speeches, rallying the masses to join the struggle for freedom and resist colonial oppression. Azad's ability to inspire others with his fervent patriotism and unwavering commitment to the cause galvanised great support for the independence movement in Jhansi. He also acquired his driving skills at the Bundelkhand Motor Garage in Sadar Bazar while residing in Jhansi.

Understanding the value of developing future leaders for the freedom cause, Azad made it his mission to teach and advise the next generation of revolutionaries in Jhansi. He instilled the virtues of bravery, resiliency, and selflessness in the following generation of liberation fighters by sharing his knowledge and experience with them. Azad used to give a book called "The Indian War of Independence 1857" (written by Veer Savarkar) to the young generations and made it mandatory for them to read. The guidance provided by Azad would be crucial in determining how India's independence movement unfolded in the following years. He was in frequent communication with Sadashivrao Malkapurkar, Vishwanath Vaishampayan, and Bhagwan Das Mahaur, who all joined his revolutionary organisation. Azad was also close to Raghunath Vinayak Dhulekar and Sitaram Bhaskar Bhagwat, the leaders of the Congress at the time.

In addition, he lodged at the homes of Bhagwat in Nagra and Master Rudra Narayan Singh in Nai Basti. Despite his best efforts, Chandrashekhar Azad faced numerous challenges and setbacks during his time in Jhansi. The constant threat of British surveillance and informants posed a grave danger to his underground activities, forcing him to operate in secrecy and anonymity. Moreover, internal divisions and ideological differences within the independence movement tested Azad's leadership and resolve, requiring him to navigate complex political dynamics with skill and diplomacy.

Meeting the Young 'Guns' and The Revival of the H.R.A...

It's 1926, and now, the news of the daring Kakori Train Action, and its 'most dangerous-wanted man' - the elusive Chandrashekhar Azad, has captured the imagination of many young aspiring revolutionaries in India. One such revolutionary was a tall, well-built & handsome Sardar from Lyallpur, Punjab. He was young, and he was about to get married but he had already informed his parents that his only 'bride' was going to be the 'ultimate freedom of the motherland', and the one who had become famous due to his staunch patriotic ideas at the National College in Lahore. His name? Bhagat Singh! Bhagat Singh was mostly involved in writing and editing for Amritsar-based Urdu and Punjabi publications. He also contributed to inexpensive booklets that were produced by the "Naujawan Bharat Sabha" and denounced the British. Additionally, he contributed a small piece to the Delhi-based daily "Veer Arjun" and wrote for "Kirti", the periodical of the Workers and Peasants Party ("Kirti Kisan Party"). He frequently went under aliases, using names including "Balwant" "Ranjit" and "Vidhrohi".

Disillusioned with the non-violent movement and yearning for a more radical approach, Bhagat Singh was also drawn to the HRA's ideology of armed resistance. Bhagat Singh had reached Delhi by this time and he was fueled by a desire to meet the 'free man' of the Kakori action and thus, vows to find Chandrashekhar Azad. Reaching Azad wouldn't have been a straightforward task. The HRA operated in a shroud of secrecy, wary of British informants and infiltrators. Bhagat Singh sought guidance from established revolutionaries in Kanpur, individuals who recognized his true potential and understood his yearning to join the armed struggle. These revolutionaries cautioned him about the risks involved and tested his resolve. But finally, the day arrives. Bhagat Singh, brimming with nervous anticipation, enters the designated location. There, shrouded in semi-darkness, sits Chandrashekhar Azad, a man barely older than him, but already carrying the weight of leadership and the scars of revolutionary struggle. Azad, ever vigilant, scrutinized Bhagat Singh, assessing his sincerity and commitment.

Azad grilled the young revolutionary about his reasons for joining the HRA, his understanding of the risks involved, and his willingness to sacrifice everything for the cause of freedom. Bhagat Singh, undeterred, countered with his questions, seeking guidance on revolutionary tactics and expressing his unwavering support for the HRA's ideology! And the magic worked! They both bonded well and this initial meeting marked the beginning of a mentor-mentee relationship that would become a cornerstone of the HRA. Azad, seasoned and battle-hardened, recognized the raw potential in Bhagat Singh. Throughout several discussions, Azad outlined the HRA's philosophy clearly, emphasizing the importance of discipline, secrecy, and unwavering commitment. He also discussed the importance of organization, logistics, and bomb-making techniques - the crucial skills needed for a successful revolutionary act. The bond between Azad and Bhagat Singh wasn't a singular connection. They were part of a larger collective bound by a shared revolutionary purpose. They worked alongside other young revolutionaries like Shivaram Hari Rajguru, Sukhdev Thapar, and even Durga Bhabhi – a woman who defied societal norms to join the fight for freedom. Azad, through his leadership and strategic mind, became a mentor to this group, shaping their revolutionary ideals and honing their skills.

Now, around the time of the Kakori incident and the trial that followed, several revolutionary groups had formed in Bengal, Bihar, and Punjab. Following their meeting at Feroz Shah Kotla in Delhi on September 8 and 9, 1928, these groups and the HRA changed their name from the Hindustan Republican Association to the Hindustan Socialist Republican Association (H.S.R.A.) in response to the growing anti-colonial feeling. The HSRA spoke of a revolution comprising a battle by the people to establish "the dictatorship of the proletariat" and the expulsion of "parasites from the seat of political power". The socialist leanings shown in the previous HRA manifesto had gradually drifted further towards Marxism. By disseminating information and serving as the armed wing of the populace, it considered itself as leading this revolution.

Other movements of the period, such as the rural Kisan movement and instances of worker industrial action motivated by communism, aptly reflected the ideals of the HSRA. It was determined that the HSRA, which was then being reorganised from the HRA, would collaborate with "Communist International". Bhagwati Charan Vohra wrote the manifesto for the HSRA ('Philosophy of the Bomb'). Even though Chandrashekhar Azad was absent from this Feroz Shah Kotla conference, he was overwhelmingly chosen to serve as the HSRA's Commander-in-Chief.

Avenging Lala Ji's Death and a 'Failed Bombing'...

A Commission, led by Sir John Simon, was established by the British government in 1928 to provide a report on the political climate in India. Though not all of them did, certain Indian activist organisations objected to the panel since not a single Indian was on its membership list. It had the effect of bringing together disparate opposing activist groupings. The Simon Commission came to Lahore on October 30, 1928, and Lala Lajpat Rai organised a nonviolent demonstration against it. James A. Scott, the superintendent of police, gave the order for his officers to lathi-charge the demonstrators in a brutal response and specifically ordered them to assault Lala Lajpat Rai. Despite being heavily bruised, Lala Ji spoke at a meeting thereafter. However, on November 17, 1928, he ultimately passed away from his wounds, which greatly infuriated Bhagat Singh, Chandrashekhar Azad, and the other HSRA members.

They all swore to murder Scott in retaliation and to send a strong message to the domineering British government. A plot was made accordingly, and along with Azad and Bhagat Singh, other revolutionaries such as Shivram Hari Rajguru, Sukhdev Thapar, and Jai Gopal were also included. D-Day arrived (17th December 1928), and unfortunately, a blunder happened during the action. In a case of mistaken identification, Bhagat Singh was, nevertheless, told to fire when Assistant Superintendent John P. Saunders showed up instead of Scott. Saunders was shot down by

Bhagat Singh and Rajguru as he was leaving the District Police Headquarters in Lahore. Azad's covering fire killed Chanan Singh, the Head Constable who was pursuing them. The HSRA, under the leadership of Chandrashekhar Azad, had sent a shockwave through the empire, proving that the Indian freedom struggle wouldn't be quelled through violence or intimidation.

POSTER-AFTER SAUNDERS' MURDER

"Notice"
By Hindustan Socialist Republic Army.
'Bureaucracy Beware'

With the death of J.P. Saunders the assassinaiton of Lala Lajpat Rai has been avenged.

It is a matter of great regret that a respected leader of 30 crores of people was attacked by an ordinary police officer like J.P. Saunders and met with his death at his mean hands. This national insul was a challenge to young men.

Today the world has seen that the people of India are not lifeless; their blood has not become cold. They can lay down their lives for the country's honour. The proof of this has been given by hte youth who are ridiculed and insulted by the leaders of their own country.

'Tyrant Government Beware'

Do not hurt the feelings of the oppressed suffering people of this country. Stop your devilish ways. Despite all your laws preventing us from keeping arms and despite all your watchfulness, people of this country would conitnue to get pistols and revolvers. Even if these arms are not adequae in numbers for an armed revolution, they would be sufficient for avenging the insult to the country's honour. Even if our own people condemn us and ridicule us and if foreign government subjects us to any amount of repression, we shall all be ever ready to teach a lesson to foreign tyrants who insult our national honour. Despite all opposition and repression, we shall carry forward the call for revolution and even we go to the scaffold for being hanged, we shall continue to shout:

"Long Live Revolution!"

We are sorry to have killed a man. But this man was a part of cruel, despicable and unjust system and killing him was a necessity. This man has been killed as an employ of the British Government. This Government is the most oppressive government in the world.

"We are sorry for shedding human blood but it becomes necessary to bathe he alter of Revolution with blood. Our aim is to bring about a revolution which would end all exploitation of man by man.

"Long live Revolution!"

Sd/- Balraj
Commander-in-Chief, HSRA

18th December, 1928.

The escape of Bhagat Singh, Rajguru, Chandrashekhar Azad, and Durga Bhabhi from Lahore after the Saunders assassination was a daring feat accomplished through a combination of planning, disguise, and a network of sympathizers. Bhagat Singh cut his hair, shaved his beard, and donned a hat to obscure his features and look like a sophisticated Government officer. On Azad's suggestion, Rajguru disguised himself as a servant carrying luggage. Durga Bhabhi played a crucial role by posing as Bhagat Singh's wife, carrying a young child (her son Sacchidanand) to further blend in. Chandrashekhar Azad himself became a seer (a sadhu baba) smoothly escaped from the police, and fled Lahore. Eventually, Bhagat Singh, Sukhdev Thapar, Shivram Hari Rajguru and others were arrested by the police (April-May-June 1929) and went under a trial, named 'Lahore Conspiracy Case'. Again, Azad was out of reach for the police and he was still planning something 'big' in his head.

Viceroy Lord Irwin had made an ambiguous offer of "Dominion Status" in October 1929. However the majority of Congressmen and freedom fighters were not amused by this ridiculous proposal, and they demanded "Purna Swaraj" (Total Independence). Chandrashekhar Azad and the other revolutionaries, who had yet to be captured by the police, intended to take Viceroy Irwin's life to renounce this ambiguous pledge and deliver a devastating lesson to the British. A scheme to blow up the Viceroy's train was hatched in December 1929.

However, the Viceroy survived because the controller of the bomb jammed at the last second. But even for the next one and half years, Azad remained free and went underground. Meanwhile, the trial of the Lahore Conspiracy Case was going on and eventually, Bhagat Singh, Rajguru and Sukhdev were sentenced to death on 24th March 1931. Chandrashekhar Azad was now getting desperate to save these prominent revolutionary figures, or at least get someone influential to fight their case to save their lives...

AZAD Till I Die!...

In early 1931 (around January-end or February first week), intending to speak to someone credible to fight the case of his fellow revolutionaries, Chandrashekhar Azad made a visit to Ganesh Shankar Vidyarthi in Sitapur Jail at Allahabad (Prayagraj today). Ganesh Shankar Vidyarthi had previously spoken for the HRA revolutionaries involved in the Kakori Action through his newspaper Pratap. Hoping the same for Bhagat Singh and others, Azad had gone to Ganesh Shankar Vidyarthi. But because of the unfortunate restrictions that were imposed on Vidyarthi, he couldn't do much about it and therefore he suggested Azad meet Jawaharlal Nehru to help him out.

27th February, 1931, Allahabad...

Chandrashekhar Azad met with Nehru in secret at Anand Bhavan, his Allahabad mansion, to request leniency for the revolutionaries who had been given death sentences by the British authorities. To ensure Bhagat Singh's release, Azad also gave Nehru the HSRA money at that time. But in the end, Chandrashekhar Azad became highly dissatisfied and enraged and left the meeting when Nehru began to provide evasive and absurd responses. After the failed meeting with Nehru, Chandrashekhar Azad went to Alfred Park to meet his comrade Sukhdev Raj to discuss the future action plan for the HSRA.

Meanwhile, 'someone' informed J. R. H. Nott-Bower, the chief of the CID division of the Allahabad police, that Azad was at Alfred Park conversing with his assistant and buddy Sukhdev Raj. Bower phoned the Allahabad Police to come with him to the park so they could arrest him once he received it. The park was encircled by the police from all four sides as soon as they arrived. A gunfight broke out as many police officers and DSP Thakur Vishweshwar Singh stormed the park brandishing guns. In assisting Sukhdev Raj in his escape, Azad killed 3 police officers but he got badly injured in the process. Azad took a promise from Sukhdev Raj that he would continue the armed struggle for the freedom of India in the future and helped him finally escape from there. But it was time for Chandrashekhar Azad.

The odds were totally against him and he was slowly losing his breath, as he was gravely injured. In an attempt to defend himself, Azad took cover behind a tree and started shooting. The police retaliated with gunfire. Following a protracted gunfight, he shot himself in the head with the last round in his revolver, keeping to his promise to always be Azad (Free) and never be taken prisoner by the tyrannical Britishers. Not even a battalion of 80 police officers could snatch away the freedom of one man! He kept his word even when he was dying and he kept his ideals, his conscience and his soul Azad for his nation. Bower suffered injuries to his right hand and DSP Singh's jaw during the gunfight, respectively. Once the other police got to the scene, the police recovered Azad's body. The police were terrified to approach his body even after they had discovered him dead under that tree because they thought he might rise again, fight them, and flee!

The public was not notified when the body was transferred to Rasulabad Ghat for cremation. People were horrified to learn about it, were outraged, and encircled the park where the incident had occurred. They exclaimed appreciation for Azad and chanted against the British authorities. The Britishers didn't want to portray Azad as a 'martyr' and they wanted to get done with the process of the final rites of Azad. But throughout the years, Azad had gained a humungous amount of respect in the common folklore and people mourned for him and idealized him as a 'Hero', which thwarted all the plans of the British authorities to paint him as a 'Hardened Criminal'.

Azad's image as a fearless revolutionary who eluded capture for years became a potent symbol of defiance against the British Raj. His escape after the Kakori Train Action and his final stand at Alfred Park, where he chose death over surrender, resonated with the Indian public. He became an embodiment of the unwavering spirit of resistance, inspiring countless others to take up arms against British rule. Azad wasn't just a skilled fighter; he was a leader who recognized and nurtured potential in young revolutionaries like Bhagat Singh, Sukhdev Thapar, and Shivaram Hari Rajguru. He provided them with strategic guidance, and training in weaponry and bomb-making, and instilled in them the ideals of revolution and social transformation.

His mentorship played a crucial role in shaping the course of the Indian freedom struggle. The audacity of his actions, like the Kakori Train Action, served as a spark that ignited a fire of revolution across India. It demonstrated to the British Raj that the Indian freedom struggle wasn't just about peaceful protests; it was a fight for self-determination that wouldn't be easily quelled. Azad's actions inspired countless others to join the fight for an independent India. While remembered for his revolutionary actions, Azad's vision extended beyond violent resistance. Historical accounts suggest his mentorship extended to social reforms. His interactions with villagers in Jhansi highlight his concern for the underprivileged and his desire for a just society alongside an independent nation.

Chandrashekhar Azad's legacy continues to resonate in modern India. His name adorns schools, colleges, and streets, a constant reminder of his sacrifice. He is celebrated in movies, books, and folklore, ensuring his story continues to inspire future generations. He stands as a symbol of courage, leadership, and the unwavering pursuit of freedom, a legacy that continues to shape the narrative of India's fight for independence...

CHAPTER NINE

BHAGAT SINGH, SUKHDEV AND RAJGURU

23rd March 1931, 19:29 hours, Lahore Central Jail...

Within a minute, something breathtaking was about to happen! The holy land of Bharat was about to get stunned & mesmerized by the temporary standstill of the revolutionary fire that was ignited by the young compassionate Bravehearts, which had instilled fearful tremors in the hearts of the tyrant British imperialists. Heaven was about to welcome the 3 ethereal souls who had given their all for the freedom of their motherland. For ages, India has witnessed countless examples of brave, courageous and gallant people who would not think twice to lay down their lives for their Matrabhoomi and now, it was going to witness another such magnanimous moment that would be remembered till the end of the time!

"Down with imperialism... Long Live Revolution... Inquilaab Zindabaad!!!"

The walls of the Lahore Central Jail and even the authorities present there, were utterly flummoxed by these scintillating maxims delivered by a 'blazing' trio, which came from 3 different parts of India. A trio that had the sole purpose of extricating India from the shackles of the British through the means of progressive armed revolution. A trio who were ready to face death with a smile on their faces to inspire the generations to come and stand up for the divine idea of freeing India by bringing an inevitable revolution in the entire nation. This article is wholeheartedly dedicated to the behemoth contribution of Bhagat Singh, Shivram Hari Rajguru and Sukhdev Thapar in the Indian freedom struggle...

The heroics of Bhagat Singh, Rajguru and Sukhdev were undoubtedly blistering and we know of them today as the three of the most popular revolutionaries that the land of Bharat had ever produced. But the organisation that they were part of – the HSRA, or, the Hindustan Socialist Republican Army gave them the platform to implement all of their rightful strategies which in turn played a colossal role in sending chills down the spine of the British authorities. Pandit Ram Prasad Bismil gave the party its initial name, the Hindustan Republican Association (H.R.A) when he founded it in 1923. Gandhi's decision to end the non-cooperation movement in 1922 as a result of the Chauri Chaura event served as the primary impetus for the party's establishment. Younger nationalists and workers lost faith in the concept of non-violence and regarded revolutionary activities as a means of achieving freedom, while some of the leaders of the Indian National Congress broke away from it and founded the Swaraj Party. Bismil had opposed Gandhi during the INC meeting in Gaya in 1922.

With Lala Har Dayal's approval, Bismil prepared the HRA constitution in Allahabad in 1923. Sachindra Nath Sanyal and Jogesh Chandra Chatterjee, who was also a member of the Anushilan Samiti, were two more notable party members. Along with Allahabad, the HRA established centres in Agra, Kanpur, Varanasi, Lucknow, Shahjahanpur, and Saharanpur. Additionally, it had bomb-making facilities at Deogarh and Calcutta. Sanyal prepared a party manifesto with the working title "Revolutionary". It included explosive content urging the nation's youth to join the party and participate in the independence struggle, but more crucially, it disapproved of Gandhi's methods and condemned them. The manifesto called for the establishment of a socialist society in India and declared that, following the fall of British authority, it aimed to establish a "Federal Republic of the United States of India". Additionally, it called for universal suffrage and in numerous towns throughout northern India, the leaflets containing the group's specifics were disseminated covertly. Many young individuals joined the party during the years 1924-25, with prominent and iconic members like Bhagat Singh, Sukhdev, and Chandrasekhar Azad. This led to a gradual increase in the membership of this revolutionary organisation.

The Lion of Lyallpur - Sardar Bhagat Singh...

"They may kill me, but they cannot kill my ideas. They can crush my body but they won't be able to crush my spirit" – Sardar Bhagat Singh

Bhagat Singh, circa.1928

On September 28, 1907, Kishan Singh Sandhu and Vidyavati Kaur welcomed a son, Bhagat Singh, into their Jat Sikh, Punjabi household. His birthplace was Chak No. 105 in the village of Banga, Jaranwala Tehsil, Lyallpur district, Punjab province, British India. Family members of Bhagat Singh have taken part in the Indian independence movement, making them a patriotic family. The army of Maharaja Ranjit Singh was also home to some of their members. In the Punjabi Nawanshah area, Bhagat Singh's family came from the 'Khatkar Kalam' hamlet, which is close to Banga. The Ghadar Party, which was headed by Kartar Singh Sarabha and Har Dayal, included his father as well as his uncles Ajit Singh and Swaran Singh. Bhagat Singh did not enrol at the Khalsa High School in Lahore because his grandfather disapproved of the administrators' fidelity to the British government. His grandfather then enrolled him in the Arya Samaj-affiliated Dayanand Anglo Vedic High School. Several events that happened to Bhagat Singh as a child had a significant impact on him. These incidents sparked his sense of patriotism and inspired him to join the fight for India's freedom.

Then came the day of 13th April 1919 - probably, one the darkest days in modern Indian History and the worst of the British atrocities on the commoners of India - The Jallianwala Bagh Massacre! On that fateful day (it was also Baisakhi on that day), a peaceful assembly of innocent civilians, gathered to protest against the oppressive Rowlatt Act, was mercilessly gunned down by British forces. The reverberations of this heinous act shook the very foundation of India's spirit, igniting a fire of defiance in the hearts of its people. While the common folk were plunged into an abyss of grief and disbelief, the revolutionaries, their blood boiling with indignation, were galvanized to overthrow the tyrannical British Raj. The massacre was not just a massacre; it was a brutal declaration of war against the soul of India.

Bhagat Singh, then 12 years old, visited the Jalianwala Bagh massacre site, two days later. While returning home, Bhagat Singh took the soil in his jar, which bore witness to the bloodshed of the compassionately patriotic Indian masses, and took it to his home where he used to worship that jar every day! That same day, he might have taken an oath for vengeance and his eyes must've been full of rage and demanding nothing but resurrection! In 1920, Bhagat Singh joined Gandhi's Non-Cooperation Movement and openly challenged the British by burning his government-issued schoolbooks and any imported British apparel he could locate. Bhagat Singh welcomed demonstrators against the Gurudwara Nankana Sahib fire of February 20, 1921, which resulted in the deaths of numerous unarmed protesters, when he was just 14 years old.

For the protest, he warmly welcomed them to his village, and in 1922, he joined the Young Revolutionary Movement, which called for the violent overthrow of the British Empire in India. He was not a fan of Mahatma Gandhi's nonviolent ideology and lost hope after Gandhiji ended the non-cooperation movement after the famous Chauri-Chaura incident. Bhagat Singh was adamant about the fact that freedom can and should be achieved using force and the tyrant must be punished, come what may! Bhagat Singh was soon drawn to the theories of socialism after reading and researching European revolutionary movements. Additionally, he joined some revolutionary groups and swiftly ascended to become one of the organization's top leaders before changing the organization's name to the Hindustan Socialist Republican Association (HRSA).

Bhagat Singh enrolled in Lahore's National College in 1923. Throughout his time as a student, he excelled in both his studies and extracurricular activities. He was a member of the college's dramatics organisation and was proficient in English, Urdu, Punjabi, and Sanskrit. Bhagat Singh won an essay contest sponsored by the Punjab Hindi Sahitya Sanmelan in 1923. In his article 'Punjab's Language and Script,' he wrote in Punjabi and displayed a profound awareness of the issues facing Punjab.

Along with other revolutionaries, Bhagat Singh joined the Naujawan Bharat Sabha, an organisation that promotes Indian nationalism among young people. He fled from his home to Kanpur a year later when his parents pressed on marriage to avoid it (It's also largely believed that Bhagat Singh travelled to Kanpur to free the prisoners held for the Kakori railway heist but afterwards returned to Lahore for a variety of reasons). He also contributed to low-cost publications published by the Naujawan Bharat Sabha that denounced the British and wrote for and edited Urdu and Punjabi newspapers published in Amritsar. Additionally, he contributed to the Kirti Kisan Party periodical and briefly to the Delhi-based Veer Arjun newspaper. He frequently went by the aliases 'Balwant', 'Ranjit', and 'Vidhrohi'.

Bhagat Singh was detained in May 1927 under the guise that he had been involved in a bombing that had occurred in Lahore in October 1926 when the authorities got concerned about Singh's influence on young people. Five weeks after his detention, he was freed with a surety of Rs. 60,000, which was a humongous amount in those times! And then began a spree of legendary and breathtaking execution of different revolutionary activities, spearheaded by him under the banner of HSRA and under the guidance of Chandrashekhar Azad & other senior revolutionaries of that time...

The Ferocius One - Sukhdev Ramilla Thapar

Portrait of Sukhdev

Sukhdev Thapar was one of those seldom and fortunate revolutionaries who had experienced the divine aura of patriotism, right from their childhoods. The person that he had become at the time of his martyrdom was the culmination and the finetuning of all the prosperous thoughts of fighting for India's freedom from the tyrant Britishers. All of this, and yet, very little is known of him in the public domain!

Sukhdev was born on May 15, 1907, in the Punjabi town of Naughara. When Sukhdev was three years old, his modest businessman father Sri Ramlila Thapar passed away. Young Sukhdev was raised in Lyallpur by his uncle Sri Achintram Thapar, a well-known figure in society, a freedom fighter, and a follower of the Arya Samaj. When Sukhdev's uncle was detained by the British police for leading an agitation against the Rowlatt Act, he was just 12 years old. Sukhdev was affected by this episode, and his animosity towards the British government only deepened. The last straw was his uncle's second incarceration during the Non-Cooperation Movement in 1921. He was so furious about it that he was resolved to hold the government accountable for their arbitrary use of the law. Sukhdev's engagement in the Indian freedom struggle can be traced back to Lahore, where he attended the National College, a hotbed of nationalist politics, while he was a student there. Sukhdev briefly joined the Satyagraha League, a group connected to the Indian National Congress, while still in college. Later, Sukhdev met people connected to the Hindustan Republican Association (HRA), including Bhagat Singh, Bhagwati Charan Vohra, Yashpal, and others. Jaichandra Vidyalankar, a professor at his college, secretly served as the HRA's coordinator in Punjab. They were the ones who first introduced Sukhdev to the revolutionary movement which embarked on his unique journey towards the national revolutionary movement.

An Effective Leader... Sukhdev Thapar is today known as a staunch revolutionary who stood along with his brothers in this auspicious campaign of uprooting the British empire from Indian soil, but many are unaware of his unique leadership qualities which helped his respective organisations to grow in numbers! The Naujawan Bharat Sabha was established in 1926 by Bhagat Singh, Sukhdev, Bhagwati Charan Vohra, and others. Sukhdev was chosen to serve on this organization's committee. In the ensuing years, when both Bhagat Singh and Bhagwati Charan Vohra were interested in renewing the revolutionary cause, the duty of managing the organisation fell upon his shoulders. Sukhdev was elected to the central committee of the HRA (later - HSRA) and was given control of the Punjab region. In Punjab, the HSRA flourished rapidly under his direction.

Sukhdev was circumspect and took numerous safety measures when enlisting new members for the revolutionary party, providing a prime illustration of the proverb "Build in silence and let the success make noise!"...

The Fearless Marathi 'Tiger' - Shivram Hari Rajguru!

Portrait of Shivram Hari Rajguru

We only remember the bold acts of a handful of brave people, but we don't remember this young and robust lad who was not only deeply committed to the freedom movement but also did not shudder at the prospect of giving his life in defence of his motherland. He displayed unwavering courage and commitment. One fine day, when Chandrashekhar Azad questioned him about the craziness of touching a hot iron rod, he calmly said, "I'm testing myself to see if I can handle police torture!" – such was the madness that drove him from inside and made him a fearsome revolutionary of India. His name was Shivram Hari Rajguru!

In a Marathi Deshastha Brahmin family, Shivram was born on August 24, 1908, in 'Khed' to Parvati Devi and Harinarayan Rajguru. Near Pune, Khed was situated along the Bheema River. When he was only a 6-year-old child, his father passed away, leaving his older brother Dinkar to take care of the family. His elementary education was at Khed, and he then attended Pune's New English High School. Early on, he joined the prestigious 'Seva Dal'. But, once, after failing an English exam, his brother made him read a lesson to his future wife as punishment. Rajguru, at the age of just 13-14 years, who was ardently determined to do something for his nation, escaped the house with just 11 paise!

After leaving his home, he travelled to the sacred city of Varanasi (then known as Kashi), where he studied the Hindu scriptures and learned Sanskrit. He read at the Lokmanya Tilak Library in Kashi for the majority of his time there. He also went to the speeches and discussions that the Maharashtra Vidya Mandal sponsored. He memorised the "Laghu Siddhant Kaumudi" by heart and had an excellent memory. Due to his love of physical activity, he belonged to several clubs for exercise. He was connected to the Bharat Seva Mandal's gymnasium. He greatly admired Chhatrapati Shivaji and his use of guerilla warfare. He also received a gymnastics diploma (Vyayam Visharad) from the Shri Hanuman Vyayam Shala in Amravati and studied with Dr Hardikar under Seva Dal. He interacted with revolutionaries while he was learning in Varanasi.

He joined the cause and joined the H.S.R.A. in a meaningful way. He was known in the party as "Raghunath" his pseudonym. Rajguru possessed an unflinching tenacity and courageous spirit. He was close friends with Jatin Das, Sardar Bhagat Singh, and Chandrashekhar Azad within the party. He was in command of operations throughout Uttar Pradesh and Punjab, with Kanpur, Agra, and Lahore serving as his bases of operations. Rajguru was known as the party's go-to shooter because of his skill with a gun...

The Bittersweet Vengeance of the H.S.R.A!...

On October 30, 1928, Lala Lajpat Rai led a composed, nonviolent march in opposition to the Simon Commission, which had been established by the British government under Sir John Simon to assess the country's political climate. Under the orders of their chief Scott, the police severely (and deliberately) assaulted Lala Lajpat Rai as a result of the police's violent response. On November 17, 1928, he gave his last breath after succumbing to his wounds. By assassinating Police Superintendent Scott and Deputy Superintendent of Police Saunders, who carried out the lathi charge that killed Lalaji, the revolutionaries intended to exact revenge for Lalaji's death. Bhagat Singh, Jai Gopal, Shiv Ram Rajguru, and Chandra Shekhar Azad were all assigned to the project. They were preparing to murder the police chief to exact revenge on the British.

On December 17, 1928, Saunders, the deputy police superintendent, left his office and got on his motorbike. Rajguru and Bhagat Singh fatally shot him in front of the Lahore police headquarters due to a case of mistaken identity. Channan Singh, a head constable who wanted to pursue the three revolutionaries, was killed by gunfire from Azad. All of them made their getaway through the D.A.V. College grounds; the same evening, HSRA posted signs proclaiming "Saunders is dead". Posters reading "Lalaji is avenged" could also be seen all around Lahore. Rajguru departed Lahore on December 20 while posing as Bhagat Singh's servant and travelling in a first-class cabin with the revolutionary's wife and infant son, Bhagawati Charan Vohra. At Lucknow, Rajguru and Bhagat Singh split off, and Rajguru successfully went underground in Nagpur. He met Dr K. B. Hedgewar (the brainchild of RSS) and sought refuge at his place for a while. However, he travelled to Pune after a few days.

In the meantime, the HSRA was about to send Batukeshwar Dutt and Bejoy Kumar Sinha to the Central Legislative Assembly to launch low-grade smoke bombs in opposition to the proposed Trade Disputes Bill and the Public Safety Bill. Sukhdev was present at the meeting, although he rarely said anything. He allegedly got into a heated argument with Bhagat Singh after the meeting and forced him to take charge of the project. The world needed to be convinced of the revolutionaries' intentions once they were apprehended, according to Sukhdev's thesis, and only Bhagat Singh, in his opinion, had the authority to do so. Bhagat Singh granted his request, and at his request, the HSRA central committee met once more, enabling him to take the initiative in the attack that became known as the Assembly Bomb Case.

The Lahore Conspiracy Case, and the Supreme Sacrifice!...

In the Assembly Bomb Case, Bhagat Singh and Batukeshwar Dutt were apprehended and put on trial. Also, with the assistance of approvers (Jai Gopal, Phanindra Nath, and Hansraj Vohra), further revolutionaries were captured. Rajguru was detained on September 30, 1929, when he was in Pune. While he was sleeping, police found a pistol with 14 pieces of ammunition in a box nearby. The Lahore Conspiracy Case, brought by the government, ultimately named 16 people (including Rajguru). On October 7, 1930, the jury returned its verdict. Sardar Bhagat Singh, Sukhdev, and Rajguru received death sentences, while the other defendants received varying prison sentences. To get all revolutionaries treated as political prisoners (and not as criminals), along with some humane treatment, the revolutionaries began a fast within the prison. Newspapers remarked on the revolutionaries' brave and uncompromising demeanour. *'Inquilab Zindabad'* and *'Long Live the Proletariat'* were reportedly shouted as they entered the courthouse, and they sang songs like 'Sarfaroshi ki tamanna ab hamare dil mei hai' (our heart is filled with the desire for martyrdom).

Meetings, processions, and requests for the death penalty to be commuted were made. The different radical Indian National Congress leaders tried to save their lives, but they were unsuccessful. A Privy Council appeal was likewise turned down. The trio were ordered to be hanged on 24 March but were executed by hanging in the Lahore jail on March 23, 1931, at 7:30 p.m., 11 hours ahead of schedule. No magistrate was reportedly willing to preside over their hanging as required by law at the time. Instead, an honorary judge presided over the execution and signed the death orders for the three inmates whose original warrants had already run out of time. In another vile attempt by the British to demean the Indians, the three men's bodies were then covertly incinerated outside of 'Ganda Singh Wala' village by jail officials who had cut a hole in the jail's back wall. The ashes were then dumped into the Sutlej River, around 10 kilometres from Firozpur. The next day, however, their fellow revolutionaries retrieved the bodies from the cremation place and conducted a magnificent parade in Lahore.

Bhagat Singh, Sukhdev, and Rajguru were only 23 and 22 years old respectively when they died as martyrs! Every countryman will always be grateful to these heroes of the nation for their eternal sacrifice, and their spirit of giving their lives in service to the homeland will serve as an inspiration to future generations, because, **"Even if the bodies die, the ideas don't!"**

CHAPTER TEN

SURYA SEN

11th August, 1908, Muzaffarpur...

The area surrounding the prison began to fill up well in advance of the appointed hour of six in the morning. Individuals carrying floral garlands occupied the front rows of the assembly. Near Khudiram, lawyer-journalist Upendranath Sen of the Bengali news daily "Bengali" reports arriving at the scene by 5 AM in a car equipped with all the required clothing and funeral preparations. Following the hanging, police officers lined the main thoroughfare to keep back the throng as the funeral procession passed through the city. As the carriage went by, the crowd continued tossing flowers at Khudiram's body and the whole region was shell-shocked by the roars of "Khudiram Amar Rahe!!!"...

The monsoon rains of 1908 lashed against the mud walls of Noapara village, a symphony of drumming on thatched roofs. Inside a small, flickering oil lamp cast dancing shadows on 14-year-old Surya Kumar Sen's face. Curled up with a worn copy of Yugantar, a revolutionary publication, Surya devoured every word. A headline screamed: *"Khudiram Bose, Martyr for Freedom, Hanged by British Raj!"* Surya's heart pounded a frantic rhythm against his ribs. Khudiram wasn't just another name; he was a legend. A fiery teenager, only 4 years older than Surya, who had dared to challenge the mighty British Empire. The details of the failed assassination attempt and Khudiram's stoic defiance in the face of death gave the young Surya goosebumps.

Khudiram's story wasn't just about violence; it was about a burning desire for freedom. It resonated with the simmering discontent Surya felt towards the British rule that choked his homeland. He saw the arrogance of the white officials, the poverty gnawing at his village, and the stifled dreams of his people. Khudiram's act, though tragic, had become a spark, igniting a blaze within Surya. The following days were a blur. Surya haunted the local tea stall, a hotbed of hushed whispers and covert meetings. He listened, wide-eyed, as fiery orators spoke of overthrowing the British. He devoured revolutionary literature, his young mind absorbing tales of sacrifice and rebellion. Names like Aurobindo Ghosh and Bagha Jatin became his heroes...

Surya Sen! The lion of Chittagong and the beloved Masterda of the common folklore. The day when Surya Sen made his supreme sacrifice (12th January 1934), there was a revival of deep-seated hatred for British imperialism throughout the entire country. Rabindranath Tagore, Saratchandra Bose, Netaji Subhash Chandra Bose, Vinayak Damodar Savarkar and others were alive when *Master Da* Surya Sen was hanged. They were all taken aback.

That was a day unlike any other - one of immense suffering and pain for everyone in Bengal and the then-unified India when the order to hang him was formally declared. Every house and hearth was drenched in tears on the day of the hanging. For a few days thereafter, several homes in the Chittagong region stopped cooking time as a way to show their sadness. Such was an impact, respect and love of everyone towards Surya Sen.

He was leaving a great legacy behind the moment he entered the gates of heaven. Surya Sen used to always quote - ***"Humanism is a special virtue of a Revolutionary"***, and he always lived his life living up to this quote. But how did it all begin? Why, even today, do the people of Chittagong (now Chattogram) widen their chests with enormous pride when they hear the name of Surya Sen? To begin with, we have to go back to 1894...

'Master Da' Surya Sen

Formative Years of Surya Kumar Sen...

The year is 1894. The air in Noapara, a quaint village lodged in the lush Chittagong district (present-day Bangladesh), hummed with the symphony of crickets and the gentle murmur of the Feni River. Here, in a traditional Bengali household, a ray of sunshine named Surya Kumar Sen, or 'Kalu' as he was affectionately called, arrived on March 22nd. His father, Ramaniranjan Sen, a teacher with a gentle demeanour, cradled the newborn, his heart swelling with pride. Little did he know, the child in his arms would one day ignite a fire for freedom that would scorch the fabric of British rule in India. Noapara's lush pastures and swaying palms were the setting for Surya's early years. His days were colourful strands of rural life weaved into a tapestry. The koel bird's soothing notes signalled him to get out of bed in the mornings. His buddies would laugh loudly as they chased butterflies around the mango groves. He spent the afternoons skipping stones and spinning stories with the shimmering water along the riverside. The nights were a time for storytelling - his grandmother, her voice a soothing lullaby, would weave tales of old heroes and their valorous exploits. Unknowingly, these tales planted the seeds of bravery and morality in the heart of young Surya.

Ramaniranjan, a man of great moral character, taught Surya the value of social justice and education. He encouraged his son to inquire and explore, feeding his natural curiosity. As a gifted youngster with a voracious appetite for information, Surya gobbled up any book he could get his hands on. His instructors were impressed by his keen intellect and steady attention as he succeeded in his studies at the local primary school. But there was more to life in Noapara than just sunlight and jokes. Words of a far-off conflict - the struggle to free India from British domination - even permeated the sleepy hamlet. These whispers lit a fire under Surya's impressionable mind. He was desperate to comprehend what it meant to be free, the unfairness of colonial control, and the sacrifices made by revolutionaries.

The year 1912 was a turning point. The bright-eyed adolescent Surya was admitted to the exclusive Chittagong National High School. He started a new chapter in a busy town after leaving the cosy, well-known Noapara. His already developing political consciousness was further heightened by the city's multicultural population and exposure to fresh perspectives. Bengal at the time was becoming a major centre for revolutionaries, but it was still engulfed in the aftermath of the senseless bloodshed and horrific riots that had broken out after Bengal's 1905 partition. However, the most significant influence on Surya's life came during his college years. In 1916, he enrolled in the Berhampore College (now Krishnath College) in Murshidabad for a Bachelor of Arts. Here, fate introduced him to a charismatic teacher named Satishchandra Chakrabarti. Satishchandra, a revolutionary himself, was deeply involved with the Jugantar party, a clandestine organization advocating armed resistance against British rule. Recognizing the spark of rebellion in Surya, Satishchandra became his mentor. He introduced him to the ideology of revolutionary nationalism, igniting a passion that would forever alter the course of Surya's life.

With unflinching devotion, Surya absorbed revolutionary principles like a sponge. He attended meetings in secret, his youthful idealistic enthusiasm igniting his dedication to the cause. His constant companions were the revolutionaries' stories of sacrifice, their steadfast spirit serving as a light for him to follow. He exercised self-control, developing his physical and mental toughness to be ready for the battle that lay ahead. Nor did Surya forget his origins. He was a different young man when he returned to

Noapara for his holidays. By imparting his newly acquired information to his comrades, he would fan the embers of revolution inside them. Beneath the watchful eye of the banyan trees, he orchestrated secret gatherings in the village's quieter corners, where his leadership abilities blossomed.

From Master Da to a Revolutionary...

It is 1918. The world had changed, and the effects of World War I had hardly subsided. After graduating from college with a BA and a strong desire to make a difference, Surya went to Chittagong, which would later serve as the testing ground for his revolutionary zeal. Surya wasn't simply a name in the throng. The words of freedom that had become his constant companions, together with the values he had learnt at Berhampore College, were taken with him. Chittagong has a distinct vitality due to its strategic position and varied populace. This is where the struggle for independence was a tangible current that ran through the streets, not some far-off echo. His first stop was the National School, a bastion of nationalist ideals. Stepping into the classroom, he wasn't just 'Surya' anymore. To his students, he became 'Master Da' - a title that carried with it a sense of respect and authority. Master Da's classroom wasn't just a place of learning; it was a stage where he ignited young minds with the ideals of nationalism. He wove lessons in history and mathematics around the struggle for freedom, subtly planting seeds of rebellion in fertile ground. But Surya's ambitions soared beyond the confines of the classroom. He understood the power of collective action.

The Non-Cooperation Movement, spearheaded by Gandhi, was gaining momentum across India. Surya also had actively begun participating in protests and boycotts. He led marches through the bustling streets of Chittagong, his charismatic voice stirring the hearts of the masses. The city resonated with the chants of "Swaraj" (self-rule), each syllable a testament to the growing yearning for freedom. However, as the movement progressed, frustration began to simmer within Surya. He witnessed the brutal tactics employed by the British Raj to quell dissent. The Jallianwala Bagh massacre (13th April 1919) also left a deep scar on his psyche, shattering his faith in the efficacy of peaceful resistance. He longed for a more forceful move, for a spark that would spur a revolution across the country.

This disillusionment coincided with a fateful encounter. Ambika Chakrabarty, a fiery revolutionary with links to the Jugantar Party, entered Surya's life. Ambika recognized the simmering discontent within Surya and became his confidante. He introduced him to the world of underground revolutionary activities, igniting a spark that would forever change the course of Surya's life. Torn between his belief in non-violence and the growing desperation for action, Surya grappled with a difficult decision. The turning point came in 1924. The arrest of Deshbandhu Chittaranjan Das, a prominent leader of the Indian National Congress, triggered a wave of anger across the nation. In Chittagong, Surya couldn't remain a passive observer. He, along with Ambika, led a daring raid on the British-owned Assam-Bengal Railway treasury. The act not only provided much-needed funds for the revolutionary movement but also sent a powerful message - the fight for freedom wouldn't be easily extinguished!

This act of rebellion had repercussions. Ambika and Surya were both taken into custody and given 2-year jail terms. Surya's inner fire persisted despite the tough jail surroundings. Quite the contrary - it was a crucible that strengthened his commitment. He studied revolutionary theories, developed his leadership abilities, and plotted with other revolutionaries.

By 1928, Ambika and Surya had been let out of jail. Chittagong gave them a rather nervous but appraising greeting. But Surya was a different person. With the arrival of a resolute revolutionary leader, the beloved Master Da had faded into the background. When he realised that nonviolent demonstrations had their limitations, he broke up his relationship with the National School. Rather, his attention was directed towards creating a network of aspiring revolutionaries.

To build the now-famous Chittagong group, he personally selected idealistic and driven people like Ganesh Ghosh, Lokenath Bal, and Ananta Singh. Surya, with his charisma and strategic mind, became the undisputed leader of this band of revolutionaries. Surya's leadership wasn't characterized by brute force. He understood the importance of ideology and instilled unwavering loyalty to the cause in his followers. He trained them in guerilla warfare, bomb-making, and self-defence, transforming them from passionate youth into a potent revolutionary force.

The year 1930 marked a turning point in India's freedom struggle. Surya Sen, inspired by the revolutionary ideologies of Bhagat Singh and Chandrashekhar Azad, envisioned a bolder strategy: the Chittagong Armoury Raid! He meticulously planned the attack, aiming to capture arms and cripple the British military presence in the region...

A Night of Chaos: The Chittagong Armoury Raid...

The sultry night of April 18th, 1930, clung to Chittagong like a shroud. An invisible tension crackled in the air, a precursor to the storm that was about to erupt. In a dimly lit room, a band of young revolutionaries, their faces etched with a mixture of nervousness and resolve, huddled around their leader - Surya Sen. Months of meticulous planning culminated in this single, fateful night - the Chittagong Armoury Raid. Surya, his voice a low rumble, laid out the audacious plan. Their objective was simple yet daunting: capture the armouries of the police and auxiliary forces, seize their weapons, and cripple the British military presence in the region. This act, they hoped, would spark a nationwide rebellion, a tidal wave of defiance that would sweep away the shackles of colonial rule.

The revolutionaries were a peculiar group, just out of their teens and early twenties. The man spearheading the assault on the Police Armoury would be Ganesh Ghosh, a feisty young man whose commitment to the cause was undeniable. A formidable marksman with steely nerves, Lokenath Bal would lead the attack on the Auxiliary Force Armoury, a storehouse of formidable rifles and Lewis guns. Each of the remaining parties had a crucial role in causing chaotic confusion among the British by cutting off communication routes, halting train operations, and setting up detours. Holding its breath, Chittagong watched the clock reach midnight. The revolutionaries sneaked out of their hiding place, covered in darkness and equipped with a powerful combination of handmade explosives and revolutionary fervour. They were walking through the maze-like streets, their pulses pounding madly against their ribs, and the only sound that broke the tense quiet was the regular chirping of crickets.

Ganesh Ghosh and his group initially approached the Police Armoury. They overpowered the guards and took control of the building with a well-planned attack. They felt a rush of relief sweep over them, knowing that the first part of their bold plan was now fulfilled. Their celebration, though, was fleeting. They came to the heartbreaking realisation that the arsenal was empty. A potentially lethal blow had been inflicted by a critical omission in their well-planned operation. Meanwhile, Lokenath Bal and his group faced a different predicament.

The imposing gate of the Auxiliary Force Armoury seemed to mock their efforts. Precious minutes ticked by as they grappled with the sturdy barrier. Finally, with a resounding boom that echoed through the night, the gate yielded, granting them access to the armoury. Here, fortune smiled upon them. Rows upon rows of gleaming rifles and ammunition lay before their eyes - the tools necessary to ignite their rebellion. After raising the Indian National Flag on the armoury grounds, they made their getaway.

The sleeping metropolis was rocked by news of the assaults that quickly spread like wildfire. Chittagong's once-calm streets descended into anarchy. The normally a million-star night sky was suddenly filled with bursts of gunfire and explosions. Unaware of the magnitude of the rebellion, fear engulfed the British authorities. Since the revolutionaries had successfully cut off all means of communication, the city was cut off from the outside world. Trains screeching to a standstill, their tracks destroyed by Surya's troops, severely delaying British attempts to organise a counterattack.

A unit of the British Indian Army encircled a significant portion of the rebel force on Jalalabad Hill a few days later. 12 revolutionaries were martyred in the subsequent battle, many more were taken into custody, and others, including Surya Sen, were able to escape. As a skilled tactician, Surya understood the constraints of their circumstance. The British Raj was a powerful force with better resources, and it would be difficult to defeat. He made the crucial choice to withdraw to the shelter of the Chittagong hills with a sorrowful heart. This isolated and densely wooded region, full of untamed life and dangerous landscapes, provided a makeshift haven from the unrelenting British hunt. The rebels set off on a difficult journey into the unknown, carrying the weight of their daring deed as well as their captured weaponry.

Even while the Chittagong Armoury Raid's goal of inciting a national insurrection eventually failed, it accomplished something far more important. It was a powerful representation of the seething unrest in India. These youthful revolutionaries' daring and their persistent rejection of the powerful British Raj struck a chord throughout the country and caught the attention of the worldwide press. Newspapers all across the world heralded them as heroes, drawing attention to the rising discontent in British India.

The Shadow of Betrayal: The Fall of Surya Sen...

With a trail of defiance and smoke in their wake, Surya Sen and his group of revolutionaries' daring act had sent shockwaves across the British Raj. Desperate to apprehend the elusive leader, the British authority responded by placing a substantial prize of 10,000 taka on Surya Sen's head. Now a man on the run, Surya disappeared into the complex network of supporters and other rebels that spanned Chittagong. His days were spent in a never-ending dance of peril and a valiant struggle to survive under the British Raj's increasing hold. Seeking comfort in the cosy familiarity of loyalty, he took sanctuary in the modest home of a reliable friend.

But unknown to Surya, a shadow of betrayal lurked nearby. Netra Sen, a relative residing close to Surya's hideout, harboured a secret greed that gnawed at him like a hungry rat. The hefty bounty offered by the British flickered in his mind, a tempting sum that promised a life beyond his wildest dreams. The weight of kinship, the loyalty one owed to blood, meant little against the glittering allure of wealth. In a moment of unimaginable betrayal, Netra Sen approached the British authorities, his voice trembling not with fear but with the anticipation of ill-gotten gain. The betrayal was swift and devastating.

Armed with Netra Sen's information, a contingent of British police descended upon Surya's hideout under the cloak of darkness. The once-quiet house echoed with the thunderous crash of the door being broken down. Surya, startled awake, found himself surrounded by armed men, his dreams of freedom shattered by the treachery of a relative. In February 1933, Surya Sen was arrested by the British-Indian Police of the Chittagong division.

The capture of Surya Sen, a symbol of rebellion, was a public relations coup for the British. Newspapers trumpeted the news, hailing it as a victory over the forces of anarchy. However, beneath the surface, a wave of anger and disillusionment swept through Chittagong. The betrayal by Netra Sen, a man bound by blood to the revolutionary leader, left a bitter taste in the mouths of many. However, before the British could award Netra Sen, a rebel by the name of Kironmoy Sen broke into his home and used a "da" (a weapon that resembles a long knife) to decapitate him. Netra Sen's wife never revealed the identity of the revolutionary who killed her husband since she was a strong supporter of Surya Sen and his ideas. The consequences of Netra Sen's actions were severe. The once-respected member of the family became an ostracized figure, forever marked by the stain of betrayal. His actions cast a long shadow over his family, a constant reminder of the devastating impact of his decision.

The anecdote of Surya Sen's capture is a stark reminder of the complexities of human nature. It is a tale of courage and defiance juxtaposed against the corrosive power of greed. While Surya's act of rebellion ignited a fire for freedom, Netra Sen's betrayal serves as a chilling cautionary tale, a testament to how easily loyalty can be tarnished by the lure of personal gain...

The Gruesome Torture, The Martyrdom and the Legacy...

The damp walls of the Chittagong jail seemed to seep despair, a fitting backdrop for the unfolding tragedy. Surya Sen, the revolutionary who had dared to challenge the British Raj, awaited his fate. But before the final curtain fell, he was forced to endure a brutal ordeal - torture at the hands of the very people he defied. Surya wasn't alone in this crucible. His comrade-in-arms, Tarakeswar Dastidar, shared his cell and his suffering. The once vibrant revolutionaries, who had dreamt of a free India, were now mere shadows of their former selves, their bodies bearing the gruesome marks of torture. Newspapers declared Surya Sen's capture a victory, but the jubilant headlines couldn't mask the desperation of the British. The Chittagong Armoury Raid, a bold act of defiance, had rattled the colonial administration. Capturing Surya wasn't enough - they craved information, names, and details of the revolutionary network. And so, they resorted to their most barbaric tool - torture.

The methods employed were as varied as they were cruel. Sleep deprivation became Surya's constant companion. Days bled into nights, the flickering oil lamp his only source of light in the suffocating darkness. His captors, their faces shrouded in shadows, bombarded him with relentless questioning, hoping to break his spirit. Physical pain became a grim reality. Surya's cell echoed with the sickening thud of fists connecting with flesh. Whips, instruments of unimaginable cruelty, lashed out, leaving raw, burning welts on his back. They targeted his limbs, the source of his strength, twisting and contorting until pain became a dull roar in his ears. But the most insidious torture was psychological. They taunted him with fabricated stories of captured revolutionaries, whispering of betrayals and confessions that never occurred. They dangled the promise of leniency in exchange for information, exploiting his concern for his comrades.

Surya, though battered and bruised, refused to yield. He understood the game they were playing. His silence, a defiant act of resistance, infuriated his captors. They escalated their brutality, pushing him to the brink of physical and mental collapse. But amidst the pain and despair, Surya clung to his ideals. Memories of his revolutionary comrades, and their unwavering commitment to freedom, fueled his resolve. He wouldn't let them down, wouldn't betray the cause they held so dear. Days turned into weeks, the torture becoming a monotonous symphony of pain. His once strong frame grew gaunt, his eyes reflecting a deep well of suffering. But his spirit, though battered, remained unbroken. He recited poems of freedom fighters in his mind, their words a source of strength, a reminder of the bigger fight for his nation's independence. Surya, however, wasn't built to crumble. Despite the agonizing pain wracking his body, his spirit remained unbroken. He refused to utter a single word that could betray his comrades or compromise the cause. His silence, a testament to his unwavering resolve, must have infuriated his captors.

Despite their best efforts, the British failed to extract any information from Surya. His unwavering defiance, a testament to the strength of his convictions, became a legend amongst the prison inmates. He emerged from the torture chamber a changed man, his body bearing the scars of physical abuse, but his spirit undimmed. The news of Surya's torture spread like wildfire through Chittagong. Anger and resentment boiled over, further fueling the fight for independence. The British, despite their brutality, had achieved the opposite of their desired outcome. Surya Sen, the tortured but unbroken revolutionary, became an even more potent symbol of resistance.

On January 12th, 1934, Surya Sen, along with Tarakeswar Dastidar, walked to the gallows with heads held high. Their bodies were broken, but their spirits remained unconquered. Their sacrifice, along with the untold story of their torture, became a powerful rallying cry for the freedom fighters, a sturdy reminder of the price paid for India's liberation. Just a few days before his supreme sacrifice, he had written a beautiful, yet sentimental letter to his comrades & his friends:

"Death is knocking at my door. My mind is flying away towards eternity. At such a pleasant, at such a grave, at such a solemn moment, what shall I leave behind you? Only one thing, that is my dream, a golden dream - the dream of a free India. Never forget the date, 18th of April,

1930, the day of the Eastern Rebellion in Chittagong. Write in red letters in the core of your hearts the names of the patriots who have sacrificed their lives at the altar of India's freedom"...

Surya Sen's story is not just about the audacity of the Chittagong Armoury Raid, but also about the resilience of the human spirit in the face of unimaginable cruelty. It is a testament to the unwavering commitment to freedom that ultimately led to India's independence, a victory fueled not just by acts of rebellion, but also by the silent suffering endured by those who refused to be broken. Surya Sen's capture, torture, and eventual execution solidified his status as a martyr.

His unwavering defiance in the face of brutality became a potent narrative, reminding Indians of the sacrifices necessary to achieve freedom. His story wasn't just about victory; it was a stark reminder of the price one had to pay for liberty. Surya Sen's story didn't remain confined to India's borders. The international press took notice of the Chittagong Armoury Raid, highlighting the growing unrest within British India. It served as a reminder to the world of the rising tide of nationalism challenging colonial rule across the globe.

Surya Sen's legacy isn't a singular image, but a multifaceted tapestry woven with threads of courage, sacrifice, and unwavering dedication. He is a symbol of defiance that continues to inspire generations to fight for their dreams and strive for a better tomorrow. Vande Mataram!

CHAPTER ELEVEN

PRITILATA WADDEDAR

India's history is replete with the blood of many patriots and revolutionaries who gladly gave their lives in defence of their country. In addition to the men, women have made equal contributions to the independence movement, both via nonviolent and violent means. During the revolutionary era of our independence movement, Pritilata Waddedar, the first female martyr of India's freedom struggle, deserves recognition for her extraordinary bravery and selflessness at the young age of 21. She's turned into a historical legend. Pritilata's devotion extended beyond the fight for India's independence; via her acceptance of death, she hoped to demonstrate that women were just as capable as men of contributing to the cause of the homeland.

Beginning in the 1920s, there were initial attempts to include women in the national movement. Chittaranjan Das founded the *Nari Karma Mandir* in 1921 to train women for national service, while Subhas Chandra Bose established the *Mahila Rashtriya Sangha*, a political organisation, in Calcutta in 1928. The 'All Bengal Young Men's Association' changed its name to the 'All Bengal Youth Association' that same year to also allow women to join.

India's women were invited to actively join the civil disobedience campaign by M.K. Gandhi on April 10, 1930. Women could help the country by sharing men into action, spinning, and picketing foreign clothing and booze stores. This call had an incredible reaction. Thousands of women braved being fired from their jobs and lathes by the police to demonstrate in the streets and fill jails. As a result, women were able to participate in nationalist politics for the first time. Thus, women's roles and involvement in the violent Revolutionary movement changed drastically during the

1930s. This time, women were playing more than just supporting roles - they were aiming the governors and magistrates with pistols!

The Bengali youth were electrified by the Chittagong raids, which were led by Masterda (Surya Sen) during this period of widespread militancy. The infamous sign "Dogs and Indians are not allowed" at the Pahartali European Club in 1932 was drawn by Surya Sen as part of an attack. He gave Pritilata leadership of a group of 7 members on September 23, 1932, so they could stage their protest in the Club. Team members were told to bring potassium cyanide with them so they could eat it if they were arrested by the authorities in case they were stranded.

The assault proved successful. Several English club members lost their lives in the encounter. However, Pritilata gave the members the order to leave, and despite having the chance to flee, she took potassium cyanide and killed herself.

"Women today have taken a firm Resolution that they will not remain in the background... I earnestly hope that our sister would no longer nurse the feeling that they were weak... with this hope in my heart, I am proceeding to day for self-immolation", was written on a piece of paper that was found in her shirt pocket. Pritilata, was truly a lioness to the core and her true nature was reflected in such situations.

Pritilata Waddedar - The First Female Martyr of the Indian Armed Revolutionary Struggle

A Tranquil Childhood, and Growing Years...

Pritilata was born on May 5, 1911, in Dhalghat village, Patiya upazila, Chittagong (now in Bangladesh), into a middle-class Bengali Baidya Brahmin family. A progenitor of the family who had formerly gone by the surname Dasgupta was given the title 'Waddedar'. Her mother Pratibhamayi Devi was a homemaker, while her father Jagabandhu Waddedar worked as a clerk for the Chittagong Municipality. Madhusduan, Pritilata, Kanaklata, Shantilata, Ashalata, and Santosh were the couple's six children. Pritilata went by the name 'Rani' for short. Jagabandhu made an effort to provide their kids with the most education possible. He managed to get Pritilata admitted to Chattogram's Dr. Khastagir Government Girls' School.

After graduating from Dr. Khastagir Government Girls' School in 1928, she was accepted to Eden College in Dhaka in 1929. Among all the pupils from the Dhaka Board who took the Intermediate exams that year, she came in first. During her time at Eden College, she engaged in a range of social events. She became a member of the Deepali Sangha (Dipali Sangha) sect, which was led by Leela Nag and called "Sree Sangha".

On the Path of Revolution...

Her interest in politics started to grow daily throughout her friendship with Dipali and Chhatri Sangha. She once got to know Purmendu Dastidar, a Chittagong Revolutionary Party member. Pritilata demanded that Purnendu Dastidar add her to the Revolutionary Party membership list. Following a protracted discussion, Purnendu told Surya Sen about Pritilata.

Surya Sen had nothing against women taking part in revolutionary movements. He thought that women may be involved in the Revolutionary efforts, especially for certain tasks (sending covert messages, housing Revolutionaries, hiding publications that are forbidden, and offering other forms of assistance). In regards to women's involvement in direct Revolutionary action, he believed that they had not engaged in it on an equal footing with men because it involved battling the British with firearms and causing carnage. However, after learning about Pritilata's unwavering will and her readiness to engage in hands-on Revolutionary activity, Surya Sen chose to include Pritilata in his party. He instructed Pumendu to tell Priti, but that they should keep the information between them completely private. Pritilata Waddedar was therefore given the opportunity to join the Chittagong Revolutionary Party.

A brief examination of the political climate in India in the 1930s demonstrates the shift in the national movement's leaders' policies. The "Hindu Mela" foundation (founded in 1867) brought about a shift from prayers and petitions to political activism and cultural nationalism. The advent of radicalism and the revolutionary movement constituted the following stage. They were stimulated by the Swadeshi movement and Bengal's 1905 Partition. The cessation of British control was their aim. There was already a strong call for "Purna Swaraj". However, at that time, the leaders needed to prepare to issue a call for a widespread movement. Thus, they initiated the process of covert Revolutionary actions by establishing many covert organisations.

At that time, Surya Sen (1894-1934) became well-known in Chittagong as a political figure, and he joined forces with other influential people to create the Chittagong Republican Army, a revolutionary group, together with Anupam Sen, Nagen Sen, Ananta Singh, and Nirmal Sen. Their goal was to violently overthrow British control and declare the country free. The Chittagong Armoury Raid, led by Surya Sen, occurred on April 18, 1930. The raid was followed by a string of valiant acts, such as the battle of Jalalabad, in which young Revolutionaries, ages 14 to 19, valiantly fought against highly trained and mechanised British forces. After fighting nonstop for 3 hours, the British were forced to retire. The conflict resulted in the martyrdom of 11 Revolutionaries. The European quarters on the bank of the Kamafuli River were the Revolutionaries' next objective. Manoranjan Sen, Rajat Sen, Debu Gupta, Swadesh Roy, Phani Nandi, and Subodh Choudhury were assigned leadership roles during this period. In the conflict at "Kalarpole", 4 revolutionaries lost their lives.

The Pahartali European Club, and the Lioness in Action...

Pritilata was now getting frustrated with the news of all of these events. She requested that she be given some significant responsibilities by the Party leaders. Finally, Surya Sen instructed her to meet with Ramkrishna Biswas regularly. Biswas was being held in Alipur Central Jail for the assassination of Tarini Mukherjee, the Chandpore Rail Police Inspector.

Since then, Pritilata has seen Ramkrishna around 40 times, revealing her identity as the latter's cousin. She had no family connection to Ramkrishna, therefore nobody could have suspected her. Later on, it becomes clear that Surya Sen had ulterior motivations when giving Pritilata his instructions. Her frequent visits to Ramkrishna, who was patiently awaiting execution in the condemned cell, gave her a renewed sense of purpose and determination for revolutionary action. Pritilata kept a journal in the past. She used to write in her notebook every day, capturing her feelings and observations following each visit. Ramkrishna Biswas was hung shortly after, which shocked Pritilata mentally.

Emotionally distraught, Pritilata did not want to waste any time following Ramkrishna's death. She now desired to actively participate in revolutionary movements. She nurtured a strong sense of patriotism as a youngster, and now she wanted to demonstrate it with action. She was driven to take action for her country after learning about the sacrifices and biographies of people like Khudiram, Kanailal, Bagha Jatin, and others. Pritilata found inspiration in Rani Lakshmi bai of Jhansi, and her resistance against the British. She was restless because of the philosophy of life she had seen in Ramkrishna (*"Jiban Mrityue Payer Bhritta Chitta Bhabana hin"*).

In a Dhalghat village shelter in June 1932, she met Surya Sen while on her expedition. During that period, Surya Sen sought refuge in the Dhalghat village in Savitri Devi's home. Alongside him were Purba Sen and Nirmal Sen. That was Pritilata's first encounter with Surya Sen. Surya Sen gave Priti the go-ahead to fight the Englishmen in Chittagong after giving it careful thought and taking note of Pritilata's bravery and unwavering determination. Consequently, the next day, Pritilata had to depart from the Dalghat Shelter. Sadly, though, the British, under Captain Cameron's command, attacked the location early on the night of the 13th after receiving intelligence about Surya Sen. Although Nirmal Sen was shot and killed by a Gorkha soldier, Captain Cameron was murdered by Nirmal Sen's bullets. Though their other comrade Apurba was killed by an enemy bullet while travelling, Pritilata and Surya Sen managed to escape the police cordon.

Pritilata went back home following the Dhalghat incident. Since Pritilata had left her garments at the Dhalghat Shelter, cops were apprehending her during this period. What she had suspected came to pass. Due to suspicions about her role in the Dhalghat incident, police visited her home. One of Pritilata's photos and her writings were found in Dhalghat. Priti's home was searched by police, but nothing indiscriminate was discovered. Priti was kept under house arrest. Priti's life became meaningless when she was at home at this time. She could not bear to be confined like this. That was the instant Surya Sen gave her the order to leave home and labour underground. Pritilata fled her home on July 5, 1932, as a result.

In the 3 months that she spent running away, Pritilata readied herself for her role in the revolution. A reward of Rs. 500 was announced by the British authorities for her apprehension. She received training this time around to handle explosives, pistols, and revolvers. The most significant day finally arrived for her long-awaited desire on September 24, 1932. Pritilata was given the go-ahead by Surya Sen to raid the Pahartali European Club with seven other young Revolutionaries - Pannalal Sen, Shanti Chakraborty, Prafulla Das, Bireswar Roy, Mahendra Chowdhury, Sushil Dey, and Kalikinkar Dey. Remarkably, the initial objective of the Chittagong Revolutionaries was to assault the European Club, where a large number of Europeans might be located, rather than individual Europeans. Thus, the Revolutionaries intended to get retribution for the British Government's horrific killing of innocent people at Jallianwala Bagh in April 1919 by assaulting the Europeans gathered together.

The D-Day...

Around 10 p.m., all of the Revolutionaries gathered near the Club under the direction of Pritilata. While the others were disguised as coachmen similar to the coachman of the club, Pritilata was dressed as a soldier. They all had revolvers, explosives, and many rifles and shotguns among their weapons. The Revolutionaries obtained comprehensive information about the club from a servant who worked there, including the number of doors and windows in the room, the access and escape routes, the number of police officers and troops on duty to defend the club's gates, etc. It was also arranged that he (the servant) would signal the revolutionaries with a torchlight from the club's kitchen window.

At ten o'clock at night, the revolutionaries entered the club and began their activity based on his signal. They staged a bomb attack on the club and opened fire while Revolvers were stationed at the entrances and windows of the structure. Inside the club, there was chaos among the European patrons. They became quite agitated. Additionally, they had nothing to do because the Revolutionaries had barred all exits.

Approximately 200 people were hurt in the ensuing altercation, and one woman was shot and killed. Pritilata commanded everyone to halt and depart from the area. She was shot in the breast abruptly and collapsed to the ground. Immediately, she decided to end her life rather than face police capture. She instructed her friend to leave the area right away, gave her pistol to them, ingested potassium cyanide, and eventually breathed her last...

Her corpse was discovered and recognised by the police the next day. When the police searched her corpse, they discovered a few flyers, a picture of Ramkrishna Biswas, gunshot wounds, a whistle, and a draft of their attack plan. The post-mortem revealed that cyanide poisoning was the cause of her death and that the gunshot wound was not particularly serious.

A Legacy that lives on...

Pritilata Waddedar's story doesn't end with her last breath. The ripples of her sacrifice continue to be felt even today. Pritilata shattered the stereotype of the docile Indian woman. Her courage in leading an armed attack challenged the prevailing notions of femininity and proved that women were equally capable of fighting for freedom. She became an inspiration for countless other women to join the independence movement.

Pritilata's story embodies the unwavering spirit of the Indian independence movement. Her willingness to sacrifice everything for her nation continues to inspire feelings of patriotism and a sense of duty towards the country. The Chittagong Armory Raid, led by Surya Sen and in which Pritilata played a pivotal role, served as a turning point in the freedom struggle. It demonstrated the vulnerability of the British Raj and emboldened other revolutionaries to take more decisive action.

Pritilata's story serves as a potent reminder that the fight for justice and equality is a continuous one. While India may have gained independence, new challenges like social injustice and economic inequality persist. Her courage inspires us to confront these issues head-on and strive to build a better nation.

As we move forward, it's vital to ensure that stories like Pritilata's continue to be told and retold. By keeping the memories of such brave individuals alive, we not only honour their sacrifices but also draw upon their strength and determination to face the challenges of our times. Pritilata Waddedar's legacy is a testament to the power of courage, a reminder that even the seemingly ordinary can achieve extraordinary feats when driven by a burning desire for freedom. Her story can serve as a timeless inspiration, urging us to fight for what we believe in and strive to create a just and equitable world!

Pahartali European Club today

CHAPTER TWELVE

SUNITI CHOUDHURY

23rd March, 1931...

The news crackled through the telegraph wires, a lightning bolt splitting the Bengal sky on this day! Bhagat Singh, Rajguru, and Sukhdev - names whispered with reverence in hushed tones - were gone. Executed in Lahore, their defiance hung heavy in the air, a bitter truth settling on the tongues of every freedom fighter. In a small town nestled within Bengal, the news found its way to Santi Ghose and Suniti Choudhury, two teenagers barely out of childhood. The worn photograph of Bhagat Singh, his eyes blazing with defiance, that adorned their secret meeting place seemed to lose its vibrancy, replaced by a hollowness that echoed in their hearts.

Suniti, usually the picture of quiet determination, slammed her fist on the rickety table, a single tear tracing a path down her cheek. Shanti, her fiery spirit banked but not extinguished, felt a cold rage simmer within. They spoke in hushed tones, their voices laced with a newfound urgency. Netaji Subhash Chandra Bose, the firebrand leader whose speeches they devoured in stolen moments, echoed in their minds. His words, a clarion call for armed resistance, resonated with a newfound intensity. In that charged moment, under the dim glow of an oil lamp, a pact was forged.

Tears turned to steely resolve. They wouldn't mourn, they would act. The hanging wouldn't be the end, it would be the spark. Avenge. That became their mantra, their silent oath whispered into the night, a promise etched in the fierce glint of their eyes.

The target, a symbol of colonial oppression that loomed large in their town - Charles Stevens, the District Magistrate – became a focal point, their act of defiance a desperate prayer for freedom rising from the ashes of Bhagat Singh's martyrdom...

Suniti Choudhury - The Youngest of 'em all!

Young Suniti Choudhury

India was going through a civil disobedience movement at the time. It was 1930. A teenage girl was watching the movement at its height, with all of its processions and arrests of men and women, perhaps just like any other girl from a typical middle-class home. The uprising, along with her other revolutionary classmates, contributed to the development of Suniti Choudhury, the youngest revolutionary woman in India.

On May 22, 1917, Suniti Choudhary was born in the Comilla area of West Bengal, which is now Bangladesh. She attended the Foyjunessa Balika Vidyalaya in Comilla. Ulhaskar Dutt was also a revolutionary from Comilla, and his acts had an impact on Choudhury. In the meanwhile, Choudhury also benefited greatly from the influence of Prafulla Nalini Brahma, her immediate senior at Faizunnisa Girls' High School. Along with providing her with books and other revolutionary literature that the British had outlawed, she also served as her tutor.

Swami Vivekanand's well-known statement, "Life is a sacrifice for the Motherland", influenced Choudhury's worldview. She also brought Suniti into the Jugantar Party. She also became a member of the female branch of the Jugantar-affiliated Tripura Zilla Chhatri Sangha.

The District Volunteer Corps appointed Suniti Choudhury as its Major. When Netaji Subhash Chandra Bose visited the city to speak to the student group, she led the females in the march. Choudhury was chosen to serve as the Women's Volunteer Corps Captain during the Tripura Zilla Chhatri Sangha's Annual Conference, which took place on May 6, 1931. She went by the moniker 'Meera Devi' during this period. As the chosen "custodian of firearms", she was tasked with instructing female members of the Chhatri Sangha in the arts of lathi, sword, and dagger play.

Prafulla Brahma questioned Netaji Subhash Chandra Bose over women's participation in direct revolutionary action while he was meeting the girls after the conference. *"I will be pleased to see you people in the front rank"*, he replied in response. ***"To preserve your honour, take up arms yourselves, YE MOTHERS"***, Subhash Chandra Bose wrote in response to Santi Ghose's request for his autograph.

In the meantime, Chhatri Sangha was educating young ladies, and the most intelligent and courageous trainees were supplying the rebels with documents, weapons, ammunition, and cash. Prafulla, Santisudha Ghose, and Suniti Choudhury, however, called for more accountable roles. They desired the same level of responsibility as males. Some top authorities understandably questioned why females were picking up guns in light of this. Suniti said, ***"What good is our current dagger-and-stick play if we shy away from real action?"*** when this occurred...

A Daring Plot and a Perfect Execution!...

In December 1931, Jugantar's leadership entrusted a dangerous mission to Santi Ghose and Suniti. Their target: Charles Geoffrey Stevens, the British District Magistrate of Comilla, a symbol of colonial authority in their hometown. The act was audacious, a testament to the unwavering spirit of these young girls.

On December 14, 1931, Choudhury, then 14 years old, and Santi Ghosh, then 15 years old, entered Charles Geoffrey Buckland Stevens' office. To go inside his office, they set up a petition to have a swimming competition among their students. Ghosh and Choudhury took out automatic handguns that were concealed behind their shawls and shot and killed Stevens while he was studying the document. Within a moment, the man who was directly responsible for the atrocities happening at the local level within Comilla was lying in a pool of blood on the floor. The revenge had been taken successfully and then, both of them were immediately arrested and taken to the local police station. Suniti Choudhury was particularly happy with her service to her motherland and avenged her brothers. Both Shanti and

Suniti were immensely satisfied that now they'd be joining their fellow revolutionaries in heaven and everyone would now pat their backs with great pride! But their dreams of joining their comrades in heaven were squandered by the authorities when their trials came...

The Aftermath: Facing the Consequences...

The capture and subsequent trial painted a stark picture of the harsh realities they faced. No longer revolutionaries, they were children thrust into the unforgiving world of a colonial court. The girls were arrested and placed in the British jail that served their community. Choudhury and Ghosh were composed and upbeat during their trial days in both the jail and the courtroom, despite all the challenges. They anticipated dying as martyrs. Nevertheless, as children, Ghosh and Choudhury were given ten-year prison sentences when they appeared in court in Calcutta in February 1932. *"It is better to die than live in a horse's stable!"*, they said in an interview.

Suniti Choudhury was detained as a 'third class prisoner' in the Hijli Detention Camp. Her family also had to deal with the fallout from her actions; her father's government pension was halted, and her two older brothers were detained without being allowed to defend themselves. After years of starvation, her younger brother passed away from consumption. After serving 7 years of her imprisonment, she was freed in 1939 together with Santi Ghose. Despite their youth, their sentence of rigorous imprisonment was a harsh reminder of the unforgiving nature of the Raj. The confines of Alipore Central Jail could not extinguish the fire within them. Accounts from fellow inmates depict them not as broken children, but as staunch symbols of resilience.

Santi Ghosh

A Legacy that Endures...

The killing of Stevens was described in modern Western journals as an indication of "Indians' outrage against an ordinance by the Earl of Willingdon that suppressed the civil rights of Indians, including that of free speech". The killing of Stevens by Ghosh and Choudhury was described in Indian media as their reaction to the "misbehaviours of the British district magistrates" who had misused their positions of authority by raping Indian women.

The Rajshahi District police intelligence division discovered a leaflet endorsing Ghose and Choudhury as nationalist heroes after the decision was rendered. Lines from Robert Burns' poem Scots Wha Hae were printed alongside pictures of the two girls on the poster, which said, *"THOU ART FREEDOM'S NOW, AND FAME'S: Tyrants fall in every foe! Liberty's in every blow!"*

After the release, Suniti Choudhury went back to school and completed the M.B.B.S. programme. She wed Pradyot Kumar Ghose in 1947. In 1988, the youngest female revolutionary of India, Suniti Choudhury passed away at the age of 70. Conversely, Santi went back to school and married Chittaranjan Das, a former Chittagong revolutionary, in 1942. For a considerable amount of time (1952-1968), Santi Ghose (Das) served as a member of both the Legislative Assembly and the West Bengal Legislative Council.

Santi Ghose and Suniti Choudhury's story is more than just a historical footnote. It is a powerful reminder that the yearning for freedom can ignite even the most innocent hearts. Their actions, while controversial, were a product of their times, a desperate act against an oppressive regime. However, their story also compels us to consider the cost of freedom. Were these young girls simply pawns in a larger game? Should their childhood have been sacrificed at the altar of revolution? Ultimately, Santi Ghose and Suniti Choudhury's story is a poignant reminder of the human cost of freedom. It is a tale of youthful idealism, unwavering courage, and the enduring spirit of rebellion that continues to inspire generations...

CHAPTER THIRTEEN

SARDAR UDHAM SINGH

The pages of history are often stained with blood and valour, tales of oppression and resistance, of pain and defiance. Among these stories, the saga of Sardar Udham Singh stands out as a powerful narrative of revenge and justice, intertwined with the broader struggle for India's independence from British colonial rule. Born into a humble family, Udham Singh's life was marked by a singular event that changed the course of his destiny - the Jallianwala Bagh massacre. This chapter delves into the life of this enigmatic revolutionary, whose mission became a testament to his unyielding spirit and unwavering determination to seek justice.

Sardar Udham Singh

Early Life, Influences and the British Indian Army...

On December 26, 1899, in the Pilbad area of Sunam, some 200 km south of Lahore, British India, Udham Singh was born "Sher Singh" into a Sikh household. His parents were Tehal Singh, a low-skilled manual worker from Kamboj, and his wife Narain Kaur. He was the youngest of their two brothers, Sadhu Singh being the older by 2 years. Their mother died when they were around 3 and 5 years old, respectively. After that, the two boys remained beside their father while he worked in the Punjab Canal Colonies, in the village of Nilowal, transporting mud from a recently built canal. He obtained employment as a railway crossing watchman in the hamlet of Upali after losing his job.

The father of the boys passed away at Ram Bagh Hospital in October 1907 while walking them to Amritsar. After being passed to an uncle who was unable to care for them, the two brothers were enrolled at the Central Khalsa Orphanage on October 28, 1907, where they were raised. Sher Singh was renamed as *"Udham Singh"* (Udham means 'upheaval'), and Sadhu became *"Mukta"*, after being rebaptized per Sikh customs. Udham was lovingly called "Ude" in the orphanage. Mukta died suddenly in 1917 from an ailment that was not known. God had a different plan for Udham Singh, as he now was the only member of his family and all of his loved ones (mother, father and elder brother were in heaven).

Not long after, Udham Singh convinced officials to let him enlist in the British Indian Army during the First World War even though he was under the required enlistment age. After that, he was sent to the 32nd Sikh Pioneers' lowest-ranking labour unit to work on field railway reconstruction from the coast up to Basra. It took him less than six months to return to Punjab because of his youthful age and issues with authorities. He re-enlisted in the army in 1918 and was sent to Basra and later Baghdad, where he performed general maintenance on machines and cars and carpentry. He returned to the Amritsar orphanage in early 1919 after a year.

The Jallianwala Bagh Massacre

The year 1919 was a watershed moment in Indian history. The British colonial government's repressive measures had reached a new peak with the implementation of the Rowlatt Act, which curtailed civil liberties and allowed for detention without trial. Protests against this draconian law were widespread, and Punjab, in particular, was a hotbed of dissent.

Several local figures associated with the Indian National Congress, including Satyapal and Saifuddin Kitchlew, were detained on April 10, 1919, following the Rowlatt Act. A military picket opened fire on a demonstrating crowd, sparking a disturbance that resulted in attacks on many European-owned banks and multiple Europeans being attacked in the streets.

On April 13, 1919, the city of Amritsar was celebrating Baisakhi, a major Sikh festival. Thousands of men, women, and children gathered at Jallianwala Bagh, a public garden, to participate in the celebrations and to peacefully protest against the Rowlatt Act. The atmosphere was festive, with people enjoying the holiday, unaware of the impending tragedy.

General Reginald Edward Harry Dyer, the acting brigadier general in Punjab, viewed the gathering as a threat to British authority. He marched into the garden with 50 riflemen, blocking the only exit. Without any warning, he ordered his troops to open fire on the unarmed crowd. The firing continued for 10 minutes, with the soldiers aiming directly at the densest parts of the crowd. The scene was one of sheer horror - people were shot in the back as they tried to flee, while others jumped into a well to escape the bullets, drowning in the process.

Young Udham Singh was present at Jallianwala Bagh that day. He and his friends were serving the water and short refreshments to the public which also included children and old folks. He witnessed the massacre firsthand, saw the dead and dying, and helped carry the wounded to safety. The sight of hundreds of innocent people being slaughtered left an indelible mark on him. It was a moment of profound trauma, darkness and a turning point in his life.

The massacre at Jallianwala Bagh was a defining moment for Udham Singh. The brutality he witnessed instilled in him a burning desire for revenge. Standing amidst the bodies of his fellow countrymen, he took a solemn vow to avenge the massacre. The words he murmured to himself that day became his life's mission:

"I will never forget this bloodshed. I will not rest until I have avenged my people".

This vow became the driving force of his existence. He knew that to achieve his goal, he needed to prepare meticulously and strategically. He joined the ranks of the Ghadar Party, an organization dedicated to overthrowing British rule in India. The party's activities took him to various parts of the world, where he networked with other revolutionaries and gathered support for the cause.

Ghadar and The Long Road to Revenge

Udham Singh's journey was not a straightforward path. It was fraught with challenges and setbacks. After joining the Ghadar Party, he travelled extensively, visiting countries such as the United States, Germany, and the Soviet Union. These travels were not mere wanderings; they were a part of his larger plan to build a network of allies and gather resources for his mission. Bhagat Singh and his revolutionary organisation, The Hindustan Socialist Republican Association, had a significant effect on Udham Singh when he got active in revolutionary activities. Udham Singh joined the Ghadar Party in 1924 and helped organise Indians living abroad to overthrow colonial rule.

In the United States, he worked alongside prominent Indian revolutionaries like Lala Har Dayal and others. He was arrested several times for his anti-British activities, but each time he emerged more determined than before. His commitment to his cause was unwavering, and he continued to plan meticulously for the day he would strike. During this period, he adopted several aliases to avoid detection by British intelligence. He was known as Sher Singh, Udham Singh, and even 'Frank Brazil' at different points in his life. These aliases were not just a means of evading capture; they were a testament to his adaptability and cunning.

In the United States of America, Udham Singh became even more closely associated with the Ghadar Party, which was headquartered in San Francisco. The party was comprised largely of Punjabi Indians who had emigrated to North America and were committed to the cause of Indian independence. The Ghadar Party's ultimate goal was to incite a revolution in India and overthrow British rule through armed rebellion.

Udham Singh threw himself into the party's activities with zeal. He worked tirelessly to spread the message of revolution, raising funds, recruiting new members, and disseminating anti-British propaganda. He also underwent training in the use of firearms and explosives, skills that would prove invaluable in his mission. His time in the United States broadened his perspective and reinforced his belief in the necessity of armed struggle against the British.

Udham Singh, while he was in the United States, had married a Mexican woman (in the 1920s). The name of Udham Singh's spouse was Lupe Hernandez. He departed the country in 1927, leaving Lupe and their 2 sons behind him. The "Johnson-Reed (Immigration) Act of 1924" allowed many other Indian males in the United States to marry Hispanic women since they would have otherwise been forced to leave.

On Bhagat Singh's orders, he returned to India in 1927, carrying with him ammunition and revolvers for 25 accomplices. He was taken into custody for illegal gun possession shortly after. The Ghadar Party periodical *"Ghadr-di-Gunj"* (which means "Voice of Revolt"), together with revolvers and ammunition, were seized. He was found guilty and given a 5-year jail term that would expire in 1931. Following his release from jail in 1931, Singh was constantly monitored by the Punjab Police. He travelled to Kashmir, from where he managed to get away from the authorities and reach Germany. He arrived in London in 1934 and secured a job there.

There began the ending of the story... Udham Singh was now in the proximity of his prime target - Sir Michael O'Dwyer! The predator was very very close to hunting down the petty and tyrannical murderer of thousands of innocents of Punjab and Indians. His dream of avenging the Jallianwala Bagh was now close and he had also started making plans on how to achieve it with no strings attached!

Laying the Trap, and Hunting Down the Prey...

The year was 1934.

London, shrouded in a perpetual twilight, pulsed with a frenetic energy. Among the throngs navigating the bustling streets was a man named Udham Singh. His past, a tapestry woven with revolution and loss, was a closely guarded secret. He had arrived with a singular purpose - to avenge the Jallianwala Bagh massacre, a wound that festered in his soul. Yet, the path to retribution, Udham soon discovered, would be a complicated one.

Michael O'Dwyer, the man Udham responsible for the Amritsar carnage, lived a life far removed from the dusty streets of Punjab. He was a ghost to Udham, a name etched in infamy, a symbol of colonial arrogance. Newspapers reported O'Dwyer occasionally attending gatherings, but concrete details about his whereabouts were scarce. Udham, a man of meticulous planning, needed to get closer. Nevertheless, Udham Singh's plan and his dream were not about to be bolstered by any family pressure and his wife also provided a rock-solid support to him and his cause, for she also knew the tyranny of the British!

He secured a job at a bustling restaurant in London's heart. Days were a blur of clattering plates and hurried conversations, but his nights were consumed by a different pursuit. He devoured newspapers, meticulously clipping articles about O'Dwyer's movements. He frequented libraries, immersing himself in biographies of historical assassins, their successes and failures etched in his mind.

Now, it was around 1937. One blustery evening, a chance encounter at a pub altered the course of Udham's mission. He overheard a group discussing a vacancy at a stately home in Belgravia. The name that dropped like a bombshell - Michael O'Dwyer!! Udham's heart hammered against his ribs. Here was his opportunity, a chance to observe the man he loathed from a distance of mere feet. The interview was a tightly choreographed performance. Udham, adopting a meek persona, spoke in clipped English, his accent thick with a foreign lilt. He downplayed his experience, focusing on his ability to remain discreet. The housekeeper who interviewed him, a stern woman with steely eyes, seemed unconvinced. Yet, a flicker of pity softened her gaze as she noted the threadbare clothes and quiet desperation in Udham's eyes. He was hired and was delighted deeply from the inside. Now was his chance to closely observe and understand O'Dweyer's routine and his overall psyche.

Stepping into the opulent Belgravia house was like entering another world. Dust motes danced in the golden shafts of sunlight that streamed through the high windows. Udham, his senses on high alert, meticulously cleaned the ornately carved furniture, his mind conjuring images of the Jallianwala Bagh massacre - the choked screams, the stench of gunpowder. The air grew thick with a sense of the past, a haunting counterpoint to the luxurious present.

Days turned into weeks. Udham, a silent observer, watched O'Dwyer from the shadows. The man who had orchestrated the massacre seemed a pale shadow of his former self. Age had etched lines on his face, and a weariness hung about him like a shroud. Udham's initial burning rage began to morph into a sense of cold calculation. He studied O'Dwyer's routines, the creak of the floorboards as he walked, the rhythm of his breathing at night. The house, once a symbol of privilege, became a potential battleground.

Yet, as days bled into weeks, a strange unease began to gnaw at Udham. He witnessed O'Dwyer interacting with his family, a flicker of warmth in his eyes as he spoke to his grandchildren. A seed of doubt, previously unacknowledged, sprouted within Udham. Was he about to take the life of a man who, beneath the facade of power, was simply a flawed human being?

The answer came in immediately! - NO. *Michael O'Dwyer was not only a flawed human being but a dark and sadistic white man who considered people with 'other' colours as racially inferior. Udham Singh was absolutely crystal clear with his conscience that the man he was about to eliminate was not a human being from the core, but a monster who needed to be slayed!*

Sardar Udham Singh now gave his resignation and he decided to do the target practice of shooting a human being. Although he had briefly served in the British Indian Army it had been years ago and now his priority was to get his hands on perfecting the art of assassination. Through his extensive network of revolutionaries, he obtained a revolver and now had started his target practice to ace it on D-Day! The day he chose - 13th March 1940 at Caxton Hall!

13th *March, 1940 - Caxton Hall, London...*

At a combined gathering of the East India Association and the Central Asian Society (now the *Royal Society for Asian Affairs*) at Caxton Hall in London, Michael O'Dwyer was supposed to give a speech. Singh had arranged a ticket to access the event and he had a book with its pages altered to resemble a pistol, and inside he was hiding a revolver. He bought this revolver at a bar from a soldier. Next, he went into the hallway and discovered a vacant chair. Once the program began, Udham Singh got more and more jubilant because he heard the names of the other guests as well - Lord Zetland, Louis Dane and Lord Lamington - the heavyweights of the British Raj were also present at this grand moment and Udham had, thus, gotten a chance to shake the roots of British Empire!!

Sardar Udham Singh now awaited the moment he had dreamt of! The moment that he was anticipating and the moment that every tormented soul of the Jallianwala Bagh was praying for. Udham Singh sat there quietly with patience for the end of the program so that he could execute his divine plan and put the demon named Michael O'Dwyer to a forever sleep! Udham knew it!... that he was made for something like this and his revolutionary brother, his best friend and his inspirational 'yaar' Bhagat Singh must be watching this over from heaven and he'd be soon ready to welcome him there, up above the sky! The heart was pounding heavily and the adrenaline was rushing like anything. And then, the speech ends! The moment is now... DO IT UDE!! TAKE THE REVENGE!! VANDE MATARAM!!! His insides screamed at him and his action then roared the very next moment!!!

Udham Singh got up from his seat and shot O'Dwyer twice as he approached the speaking stage after the gathering. O'Dwyer was nearly instantaneously killed when one of these bullets entered his right lung and into his heart. Louis Dane, Charles Cochrane-Baillie, Baron Lamington, and Lawrence Dundas, Lord Zetland, were also the other victims of the shooting. Following the incident, Singh was taken into custody right away, and the weapon was taken as proof...

Udham Singh apprehended (2ⁿᵈ from the left), 13ᵗʰ March 1940

Capture and Trial

Udham Singh's trial was a significant event, attracting attention from all corners. The British authorities were determined to make an example of him, to deter others who might be inspired by his act of defiance. Despite this, Udham Singh used the trial as a platform to express his views on

British rule and to justify his actions. Throughout the trial, Udham Singh maintained a composed and dignified demeanour. He showed no remorse for his actions and continued to assert that he had acted out of a sense of justice and patriotism. His statements during the trial resonated with many Indians who saw him as a hero and a martyr.

Singh was formally accused on April 1, 1940, of Michael O'Dwyer's murder and was placed under detention at Brixton Prison. When first questioned about his intentions, Singh said:

"I did it because I had a grudge against him. He deserved it. I don't belong to society or anything else. I don't care. I don't mind dying. What is the use of waiting until you get old? ... Is Zetland dead? He ought to be. I put two into him. I bought the revolver from a soldier in a public house. My parents died when I was three or four. Only one dead? I thought I could get more".

During his incarceration, he went by the name **"Ram Mohammad Singh Azad"**. The first three words of the name represent the three main Hindu, Muslim and Sikh groups in India, symbolizing the fact that against the British, every community of India is now united and the end of the colonial rule is near; the final word, Azad, which means "free", represents his anti-colonial beliefs.

Singh embarked on a 42-day hunger strike as he awaited his trial before being forced to eat. His trial began on June 4, 1940, at the Central Criminal Court, Old Bailey, before Justice Cyril Atkinson. St John Hutchinson and V.K. Krishna Menon were his solicitors. The attorney for the prosecution was G. B. McClure. Udham Singh finally expressed his feelings in the court:

"I did it because I had a grudge against him. He deserved it. He was the real culprit. He wanted to crush the spirit of my people, so I have crushed him. For the full 21 years, I have been trying to seek vengeance. I am happy that I have done the job. I am not scared of death. I am dying for my country. I have seen my people starving in India under British rule. I have protested against this, it was my duty".

The Balidaan and The Legacy

On July 31, 1940, Udham Singh was hanged at Pentonville Prison. His execution was carried out in the early morning hours, but news of his death quickly spread. In India, he was hailed as a martyr who had sacrificed his life for the cause of freedom. His name became synonymous with courage and defiance.

Udham Singh's assassination of Michael O'Dwyer sent shockwaves through the British establishment. It was a stark reminder of the lingering resentment and unresolved injustices that had fueled the Indian independence movement. His actions inspired countless other revolutionaries and added momentum to the struggle for freedom.

In India, Udham Singh became a symbol of resistance and sacrifice. His name was immortalized in the annals of history, and he was celebrated as a martyr who laid down his life for the cause of his people. Schools, streets, and institutions were named after him, and his story was passed down through generations as a tale of heroism and defiance.

The impact of Udham Singh's actions extended beyond his immediate execution. His assassination of O'Dwyer was a powerful statement against the atrocities committed by the British, and it brought international attention to the Indian independence movement. It highlighted the deep-seated anger and resentment that colonial rule had generated among Indians, and it underscored the lengths to which individuals were willing to go to seek justice and freedom.

Posthumous Recognition

Decades after his death, Udham Singh's legacy continues to be celebrated. In 1974, his remains were exhumed from Pentonville Prison and brought back to India, where they were received with great honour. His ashes were scattered in the Sutlej River, a gesture that symbolized his return to his homeland.

In modern India, Udham Singh's story is taught in schools and commemorated in various cultural forms. Films, books, and documentaries have been made to honour his life and his ultimate sacrifice. His birthplace, 'Sunam', has become a site of pilgrimage for those who revere his memory.

One of the most significant recognitions of Udham Singh's contributions came in 1995 when he was posthumously awarded the title of *"Shaheed-i-Azam" (Great Martyr)* by the Government of India. This honour underscored the enduring impact of his actions on India's struggle for independence.

Sardar Udham Singh's life and legacy are a testament to the indomitable spirit of those who fought against colonial tyranny. His act of vengeance was not merely a personal vendetta; it was a profound statement against injustice and a clarion call for freedom. As India marched towards independence, the sacrifices of revolutionaries like Udham Singh served as a constant reminder of the cost of freedom and the resilience required to achieve it.

His story is one of pain, perseverance, and ultimate sacrifice. It is a story that continues to inspire and resonate, reminding us that the quest for justice and freedom is a timeless and universal struggle. Sardar Udham Singh, the avenger of Jallianwala Bagh, remains an enduring symbol of courage and defiance in the face of oppression. His life and actions serve as a poignant reminder of the lengths to which individuals will go to defend their principles and the rights of their people.

Through his unwavering resolve and ultimate sacrifice, Udham Singh not only avenged the massacre of Jallianwala Bagh but also ignited a flame of resistance that would burn brightly until India achieved its hard-fought independence.

CHAPTER FOURTEEN

NETAJI SUBHASH CHANDRA BOSE

4th July, 1944, Burma...

"Friends! 12 months ago a new programme of total mobilization or maximum sacrifice was placed before Indians in East Asia. Today I shall give you an account of our achievements during the past year and shall place before you are demands for the coming year. But, before I do so, I want you to realize once again what a golden opportunity you have for winning freedom.

The British are engaged in a worldwide struggle and in the course of the struggle they have suffered defeat after defeat on so many fronts. The enemy having been thus considerably weakened, our fight for liberty has become very much easier than it was five years ago. Such a rare and God-given opportunity comes once in a century to liberate our motherland from the British yoke.

I am so optimistic about the outcome of our struggle because I do not rely merely on the efforts of three million Indians in East Asia. There is a gigantic movement going on inside India and millions of our countrymen are prepared for maximum suffering and sacrifice to achieve liberty.

Unfortunately, ever since the great fight of 1857, our countrymen are disarmed, whereas the enemy is armed to the teeth. Without arms and a modern army, disarmed people can't win freedom in this modern age. Through the grace of Providence and the help of generous Nippon (Japan), it has become possible for Indians in East Asia to be united to a man in the endeavour to win freedom and all the religious plus other differences that the British tried to engineer inside India, simply do not exist in East Asia.

Consequently, we have now an ideal combination of circumstances favouring the success of our struggle all that is wanted is that Indians should themselves come forward to pay the price of liberty. According to the programme of 'total mobilization', I demanded of you men, money, and materials. Regarding men, I am glad to tell you that I have obtained sufficient recruits already. Recruits have come to us from every corner of East China, Japan, Indo-China, Philippines, Java, Borneo, Celebes, Sumatra, Malaya, Thailand, and Burma....

You must continue the mobilization of men, money and materials with greater vigour and energy, in particular, the problem of supplies and transport has to be solved satisfactorily.

We require more men and women of all categories for administration and reconstruction in liberated areas. We must be prepared for a situation in which the enemy will ruthlessly apply the scorched earth policy, before withdrawing from a particular area and will also force the civilian population to evacuate as was attempted in Burma.

The most important of all is the problem of sending reinforcements in men and supplies to the fighting fronts. If we do not do so, we cannot hope to maintain our success on the fronts. Nor can we hope to penetrate deeper into India.

Those of you who will continue to work on the Home front should never forget that East Asia particularly Burma-form our base for the war of liberation. If this base is not strong, our fighting forces can never be victorious. Remember that this is a 'total war' not merely a war between two armies. That is why for a full year I have been laying so much stress on 'total mobilization' in the East.

There is another reason why I want you to look after the Home Front properly. During the coming months, me and my colleagues on the war committee of the cabinet desire to devote our whole attention to the fighting front and also to the task of working up the revolution inside India. Consequently, we want to be fully assured that the work at the base will go on smoothly and uninterruptedly even in our absence.

Friends, one year ago, when I made certain demands of you, I told you that if you gave me 'total mobilization', I would give you a 'second front'. I have redeemed that pledge. The first phase of our campaign is over. Our victorious troops, fighting side by side with Nipponese troops, have pushed back the enemy and are not fighting bravely on the sacred soil of our dear motherland.

Grid up your loins for the task that now lies ahead. I had asked you for men, money and materials. I have got them in generous measure. Now I demand more of you. Men, money and materials have the motive power that will inspire us to do brave deeds and heroic exploits.

It will be a fatal mistake for you to wish to live and see India free, simply because victory is now within reach. No one here should have the desire to live to enjoy freedom right now. A long fight is still in front of us. We should have but one desire - the desire to die so that, so that the path to freedom may be paved with the martyr's blood.

Friends! My comrades in the War of Liberation! Today I demand of you one thing, above all. I demand of your blood It is blood alone that can avenge the blood that the enemy has spilt. It is blood alone that can pay the price of freedom.

Give me Blood and I Promise you the Freedom! Jai Hind!

This is an iconic speech that was delivered by none other than Netaji Subhash Chandra Bose while he was addressing the Indian National Army in Burma (Myanmar). We all know the last sentence as one of the most popular slogans in India. But it becomes a matter of utmost importance to know the entire backdrop to know the 'true' importance of Bose's leadership. It becomes a matter of utmost importance to know the crux of that speech and the environment in which it was delivered!

Netaji Subhash Chandra Bose - A rock-solid personality who is responsible for the nightmares of many British authorities, a hero who is responsible for giving many patriots a golden opportunity to contribute their blood & sweat to the nation and a staunch son of the motherland who had dedicated his precious life to the nation. Although Mahatma Gandhi and Jawaharlal Nehru have received most of the credit for the triumphant end of the Indian freedom fight, Subash Chandra Bose's participation is no less significant. His proper place in Indian history has been denied to him. To topple the British Empire from India, he established the Indian National Army (Azad Hind Fauj), which earned him legendary status among the Indian people.

Some say he was martyred in a horrible plane crash in 1945 (Shahnawaz Committee & the Khosla Committee reports), some say he was arrested and taken to Siberia and then eventually tortured to death and some say that he was still alive even after independence and lived a life of a sanyasi with an alias of Gumnami Baba!

Whatever the reality may be, the fact that he was the pioneer of the aggressive independence struggle and a lion whose roar made even the mightiest of the British tremble at its core. Early in 1942, German and Indian officials in the Special Bureau for India in Berlin and Indian soldiers of the Indische Legion addressed Bose as *"Netaji"* for the first time. Today,

India proudly makes use of it, to display their love & respect towards them.

Netaji Subhash Chandra Bose

Early Beginnings & The Education...

On January 23, 1897, Subhas Chandra Bose was born in Cuttack, Orissa. His mother Prabhavati Devi was a devout and religious woman, and his father Janaki Nath Bose was a well-known lawyer. A successful lawyer and government pleader Jankinath was devoted to the British Indian government and meticulous in linguistic and legal matters. As a self-made guy from the outlying countryside of Calcutta, he had kept in touch with his roots by visiting his village every year during the puja holidays. Subhash enrolled in the Protestant European School of the Baptist Mission in Cuttack in January 1902, eager to join his five elder brothers who were already in school. The bulk of the pupils were European or Anglo-Indians of mixed British and Indian ancestry, and English was the only language of instruction used in the school. The curriculum covered Latin, the Bible, excellent manners, British geography, and British history in addition to

English that was properly written and spoken. No Indian languages were, of course, taught. Janakinath made the school choice because he wanted his sons to have perfect intonation and immaculate English since he thought that would help them communicate with the British in India.

Surprisingly, the school was in stark contrast to Subhash's home, where Bengali was the sole language spoken. His mother practised intense devotion to Maa Durga & Kali, recited tales from the Ramayana & Mahabharata and performed Bengali spiritual music. She imparted a maternal spirit to the young Subhash, who curiously preferred gardening around the house to participating in team sports with other boys and actively sought opportunities to assist others in need. His father read a lot of English literature despite being reticent and preoccupied with his career. Given that he loved writers like Matthew Arnold, William Cowper, John Milton, and Shakespeare's Hamlet, it's no surprise that several of his kids later developed similar passions for English literature.

Subhash, at 12 years old, entered Cuttack's Ravenshaw Collegiate School in 1909. Also taught here were concepts from Hindu scriptures like the Vedas and Upanishads that were not typically learned at home, as well as Bengali and Sanskrit. He continued to receive a Western education, but he started dressing in Indian garb and talking about religion. He was a jubilant, confident, and spectacular intellectual, who was also renowned for his patriotic fervour when he was a student. The great Ramakrishna Paramahamsa, Swami Vivekananda, and the then-famous Hindu novel Ananda Math by Bankim Chandra Chatterjee were all mentioned in the lengthy letters that he addressed to his mother.

He received a First Class in Philosophy from the Scottish Churches College in Calcutta after winning the matriculation exam for the province of Calcutta. Swami Vivekananda's teachings had a big impact on him, and he was well known for his patriotic fervour both as a student and as a member of society. He travelled to England in 1919 to apply for the Indian Civil Services to satisfy his parents' desires. In 1920, he took the Indian Civil Service competitive examination in England and finished fourth on the merit list. But, Subhas Chandra Bose was so horrified by the Jallianwalla Bagh slaughter that he interrupted his apprenticeship with the Civil Services to go back to India in 1921. As far as the civil services were concerned, the ICS had six open positions.

In August 1920, Subhash sat the open competitive exam for them and finished in fourth place. This was a crucial opening move. A final test including additional Indian subjects, such as the Indian Evidence Act, the Indian Criminal Code, Indian history, and an Indian language, was still required in 1921. Also, successful candidates had to pass a riding test. Subhash thought passing the ICS would be simple because he was smart and had no fear of these topics. Nonetheless, he started to have second thoughts about sitting for the final exam between August 1920 and January 1921. With his father and brother Sharad Chandra Bose in Calcutta, a lot of letters were written. Subhash once said to Sharad in a letter, *"But taking the path of least resistance is not the ideal course of action for a man with my temperament who has been consuming notions that could be considered odd... Whoever does not have worldly desires at heart does not find the uncertainties of life terrifying. Furthermore, if one is bound to the civil service, it is impossible to serve the country in the finest and most effective way"*. This reflects his fierce inner zeal to give it all for his motherland. Now, Subhash Chandra Bose firmly decided not to sit for the ICS final test in April 1921. He wrote to Sharad to inform him of this choice and apologised for the harm he would be causing to his mother, father, and other family members. *"I request to have my name removed from the list of probationers in the Indian Civil Service"* – he wrote in a letter to Secretary of State for India Edwin Montagu on April 22, 1921. The next day, he wrote to Sharad once more, saying, "I received a letter from mother stating that, contrary to what father and others believe, she likes the ideas for which Mahatma Gandhi stands. I can't even begin to express how delighted I was to have such a letter. For me, it will be priceless because it has helped me relieve some sort of mental weight!"

It's interesting to note that Subhash Bose had earlier communicated with C. R. Das (Deshbandhu Chittaranjan Das!) as well, a lawyer by profession and a freedom fighter by choice, who had reached the top of Bengali politics. Also, Subhash was strongly encouraged to go back to Calcutta by Das. Subhas Bose took his Cambridge B.A. final exams half-heartedly after putting the ICS decision behind him. He passed but was given a Third Class placement. In June 1921, he got ready to leave for India and chose to have another Indian student pick up his diploma. Then began a journey that made Subhash Bose the Netaji Subhash Chandra Bose and paved the way for him to beat the British black & blue!

'Subhash Babu', The Congress & The Foundation of the Forward Bloc...

On the morning of July 16, 1921, Subhash Chandra Bose, then 24 years old, landed in Bombay, India, and immediately got to work setting up a meeting with M.K. Gandhi. Gandhi, who was 51 years old, was the head of the non-cooperation movement, which had swept over India the year before and would later develop to gain its independence. Gandhi agreed to meet with Bose that afternoon because he was in Bombay at the time. In his description of the encounter that was written many years afterwards, Bose repeatedly criticised Gandhi. Bose first believed Gandhi's responses to be ambiguous, his objectives unclear, and his strategy for accomplishing them poorly thought out. In their initial meeting, Gandhi and Bose had different views on how to achieve independence; for Gandhi, nonviolent methods for any purpose were non-negotiable, whilst Bose believed that all tactics should be acceptable if they serve anti-colonial goals. They disagreed on the issue of goals because Gandhi antagonised authoritarian forms of government, whilst Bose was drawn to them. According to historian Leonard Gordon, *"Gandhi, however, set Bose on to the leader of the Congress and Indian nationalism in Bengal, C. R. Das, and in him, Bose found the leader whom he sought"*. In comparison to Gandhi, Das was more adaptable and sympathetic towards the fanaticism that had drawn idealistic young men like Bose to Bengal. Das launched Bose into nationalist politics.

Bose was chosen to serve as both the Secretary of the Bengal State Congress and the President of the Indian Youth Congress in 1923. Also, he served as editor of "Forward", a publication started by Chittaranjan Das. After Das was elected mayor of Calcutta in 1924, Bose served as Das' chief executive officer of the Calcutta Municipal Corporation. He was arrested and imprisoned that same year while leading a protest march in Calcutta alongside Maghfoor Ahmad Ajazi and other leaders. Bose was detained and transferred to Mandalay prison in 1925 as part of a planned "crackdown" on nationalists, where he regrettably got tuberculosis.

After being released from prison in 1927, Bose joined Jawaharlal Nehru in the fight for independence as general secretary of the Congress party. Bose planned the Indian National Congress' Annual Conference in Calcutta towards the end of December 1928. His position as General Officer Commanding (GOC) of the Congress Volunteer Corps stands out in memory. Nirad Chaudhuri, an Oxford University-Awarded author, gave a lovely account of the meeting: *"Bose established a uniformed volunteer corps, whose officers received steel-cut epaulettes, and had his outfit manufactured by Harman's, a British tailor shop in Calcutta. The British General in Fort*

William received a telegram addressed to him as GOC, which was the subject of many vicious rumours in the (British Indian) press. As a real pacifist who had sworn to never use violence, Mahatma Gandhi disliked the strutting, clicking of boots, and saluting. He later referred to the Congress meeting in Calcutta as a Bertram Mills circus, which greatly incensed the Bengalis". Bose was once more detained and imprisoned for civil disobedience a short while later, but this time he was released and in 1930, at the age of 33, was elected Mayor of Calcutta.

In 1928, Jawaharlal Nehru and Subhash Chandra Bose opposed the Domination Status proposal made by the Motilal Nehru Committee, which the Congress had appointed, and both stated that they would be content with nothing less than complete independence for India. Bose also announced the creation of the Independence League. Subhash Chandra Bose was incarcerated during the Civil Disobedience movement in 1930. Following the signing of the Gandhi-Irwin accord, he was freed in 1931. When Bhagat Singh and his allies were hanged, he protested the Gandhi-Irwin pact and opposed the suspension of the civil disobedience movement. Subhash Chandra Bose was promptly detained once more by the infamous Bengal Regulation (circa. 1932-33).

He was exiled from India to Europe after a year based on medical needs. Throughout the mid-1930s, he made attempts to create institutes in different European capitals to strengthen politico-cultural relations between India and Europe. Subhash Chandra Bose returned to India after being denied entry, disobeying the ban, he was once more detained and sentenced to a year in jail. Following the 1937 general elections, Congress took control of seven states, and Subhash Chandra Bose was set free. Soon after, in 1938, he was elected as the President of the Congress in the Haripura Session. Bose attempted to retain unity, but Gandhi recommended Bose form his cabinet. The rift also divided Bose and Nehru and he appeared at the 1939 Congress meeting on a stretcher. Pattabhi Sitaramayya, Gandhi's favoured candidate, lost to him in the presidential election. Bose was strongly backed by another great freedom fighter from Tamil Nadu, named U. Muthuramalingam Thevar during the internal Congress conflict. Thevar mobilised all South Indian votes for Bose. But, Bose was forced to resign from the Congress presidency as a result of the manoeuvres of the Gandhi-led clique in the Congress Working Committee.

On the auspicious day of 22nd June 1939, Bose formed The All India Forward Bloc, and it sought to unite the political left but found its greatest strength in Bengal, his native state. Bose's steadfast backer from the start, U Muthuramalingam Thevar, joined the Forward Bloc. Clouds of World War II were on the horizon and he brought a resolution to give the British six months to hand India over to the Indians, failing which there would be a revolt. Now, Bose called for widespread civil disobedience to protest Viceroy Lord Linlithgow's decision to declare war on behalf of India without consulting the Congress leadership when World War II broke out. Having failed to persuade Gandhi of the importance of this, Bose orchestrated large rallies in Calcutta calling for the destruction of the "Holwell Monument", which then stood at the corner of Dalhousie Square in memoriam of those who died in the Black Hole of Calcutta. He was thrown in jail by the British but was released following a seven-day hunger strike. The Crime Investigation Department now had kept watch over Bose's residence in Calcutta.

The Famous Escape, The Journey Ahead and A Mysterious Conclusion...

Subhash Chandra Bose vanished from his Calcutta home in January 1941 and travelled to Germany via Afghanistan. He sought the support of Germany and Japan against the British Empire, operating under the adage "an enemy's enemy is a friend". He started making regular broadcasts from Radio Berlin in January 1942, and India responded with great enthusiasm. Bose arrived in Singapore from Germany in July 1943. In Singapore, he took over the reins of the Indian Independence Movement in East Asia from Rash Behari Bose and organised the Azad Hind Fauj (Indian National Army) comprising mainly Indian prisoners of war. Both the Army and the Indian community in East Asia referred to him as Netaji. Azad Hind Fauj proceeded towards India to liberate it from British rule. En route, it liberated Andaman and the Nicobar Islands.

The I.N.A. headquarters were transferred to Rangoon in January 1944. On March 18, 1944, Azad Hind Fauj crossed the Burma border and was standing on Indian soil. Even when faced with military losses later, Bose was able to maintain support for the Azad Hind campaign. Bose's most famous remark, *"Give me blood, and I promise you the freedom, (Tum Mujhe Khoon do, Mai Tumhe Azaadi Dunga!)"* was spoken on July 4, 1944, during a rally of Indians in Burma as part of a motivational address for the Indian National Army. He exhorted the Indian populace to support him in his fight against the British Raj in this. The Azad Hind Government, which came to issue its own money, postage stamps, court, and civil code, oversaw the INA troops. This government was recognised by nine Axis nations, including Germany, Japan, the Italian Social Republic, the Independent State of Croatia, the Wang Jingwei regime in Nanjing, China, a provisional government of Burma, Manchukuo, and the Japanese-controlled Philippines. Of seven countries, five were authorities founded under Axis occupation. In November 1943, this government took part in the so-called Greater East Asia Conference as an observer.

Netaji was rumoured to have perished in a plane crash in 1945 while en route to Taiwan, although this has been hotly debated and never proven. Many contend that Netaji did not perish in the plane disaster. He successfully made his way to Russia, where he spent several years before going back to India. There are numerous assertions that "Subhash Chandra Bose" was the hermit known as "Gumnami Baba" who lived in disguise in Uttar Pradesh.

The history of Indian independence is replete with the valiant deeds of innumerable freedom warriors who risked all in their fight for the motherland's independence from colonial tyranny. Among all the independence fighters, Netaji Subhash Chandra Bose played a crucial part, and his significant contribution helped our nation achieve freedom.

It doesn't matter how his soul left his body, it definitely must have received the warmest welcome ever at the gates of heaven!

CHAPTER FIFTEEN

CAPTAIN LAXMI SAHGAL

December 1944, Burma...

In the dimly lit streets of Rangoon during the peak of World War II, a figure of unwavering resolve and steely determination moved with purpose. Clad in the khaki uniform of the Indian National Army (INA), she exuded an aura of authority and compassion that drew the admiration and respect of all who encountered her. This was Captain Laxmi Sahgal, a woman whose journey from a medical practitioner to a revolutionary leader in the fight for India's independence would become a testament to the unyielding spirit of India's daughters. Her story is one of courage, resilience, and an unbreakable commitment to the cause of freedom...

Captain Laxmi Sahgal

Early Life and Formative Years...

Laxmi Swaminathan, later known as Captain Laxmi Sahgal, was born on October 24, 1914, in the bustling city of Madras (now Chennai). Her father, Dr. S. Swaminathan, was a well-respected lawyer and a prominent member of the Indian National Congress, while her mother, A.V. Ammukutty, was a social worker and a staunch advocate for women's rights. Growing up in a household that fervently supported the freedom movement, young Laxmi was imbued with a sense of patriotism and social justice from an early age.

Laxmi's education was a blend of traditional and progressive influences. She attended Queen Mary's College in Madras, where she excelled in academics and developed a keen interest in medicine. This passion led her to pursue a degree in medicine from Madras Medical College, where she not only honed her skills as a physician but also cultivated a deep empathy for the plight of the oppressed and marginalized.

After her marriage to pilot P.K.N. Rao failed, she departed for Singapore in 1940. She had the opportunity to meet a few Indian National Army soldiers under Subhas Chandra Bose when she was in Singapore.

Little did she know that this decision would set her on a path that would forever alter the course of her life and that of her nation. Netaji Subhash Chandra Bose's aura was such that it could bring a dead person back to life and inspire him/her to fight tirelessly hard for the nation. The influence on Laxmi was no different! Even she got to know Netaji and that paved a beautiful way for her to begin her fight for the freedom of Bharat!

Netaji Subhash Chandra Bose's Influence & the Azad Hind Fauj

The turning point in Laxmi's life came in 1942 when she met Netaji Subhash Chandra Bose, the charismatic leader of the Indian National Army (INA), during his visit to Singapore. Bose's magnetic personality and his unwavering dedication to the cause of India's independence left an indelible impression on her. Inspired by his vision and leadership, Laxmi was determined to contribute more significantly to the freedom struggle.

When the British gave over Singapore to the Japanese in 1942, Lakshmi helped injured prisoners of war, many of whom wanted to create an Indian independence army. During this period, several nationalist Indian employees in Singapore were K. P. Kesava Menon, S. C. Guha, and N. Raghavan, who established a Council of Action. However, the Japanese occupiers made no solid promises or granted permission for their Indian National Army, or Azad Hind Fauj, to fight in the war. Subhash Chandra Bose reorganised the movement against this backdrop when he landed in Singapore on July 2, 1943.

Netaji's approach to the fight for India's independence was revolutionary. Unlike many of his contemporaries in the Indian National Congress, who advocated for non-violent resistance, Bose believed in armed struggle as a legitimate means to overthrow British rule. His boldness and strategic brilliance captivated Laxmi, who saw in him a leader who could inspire a nation to rise against its colonial oppressors.

Laxmi Sahgal, later had written beautifully about this anecdote while proving the full context about it. She wrote, *"At the second mass meeting, Netaji dropped a bombshell by saying that it was his intention to form a women's infantry regiment, named after the Rani of Jhansi who had fought so heroically against the British in 1857... I told him I was ready to join... The date was July 8, 1943"*. Women flocked to join the all-female brigade with enthusiasm, and Dr Lakshmi Swaminathan took on the name 'Captain Lakshmi' - a moniker and identity that she would carry with her forever.

The formation of the Rani of Jhansi Regiment was a bold and revolutionary step, challenging the traditional gender roles that confined women to domestic spheres. Under Captain Laxmi's command, the regiment became a beacon of women's empowerment and resilience. These women, drawn from various walks of life, underwent rigorous training and participated in several battles alongside their male counterparts. Under Subash Chandra Bose's leadership, the Provisional Government of Free India in Singapore had Captain Lakshmi as its "Minister in Charge" of the Women's Organisation.

Captain Laxmi's leadership was characterized by her compassion and unwavering dedication to her troops. She was not just a commander but a mentor and a source of inspiration for her soldiers, many of whom had never imagined themselves in combat roles. Her ability to empathize with her troops, combined with her medical expertise, made her a beloved leader who earned the respect and loyalty of her regiment.

One of the most significant moments in Captain Laxmi's military career came during the INA's campaign in Burma (now Myanmar) in December

1944. Despite facing insurmountable odds and fierce resistance from the British forces, she led her regiment with exemplary courage and determination. Her leadership during the battles in Imphal and Kohima became legendary, as she and her regiment fought valiantly, embodying the spirit of freedom and sacrifice.

In December 1944, the INA marched to Burma alongside the Japanese army. However, by March 1945, the INA leadership realised that the war was going against them and they had to return before they could reach Imphal. After being taken into custody by the British in May 1945, Captain Lakshmi stayed in Burma until March 1946, when she was sent to India. This was during the INA trials in Delhi, which increased public unhappiness and accelerated the end of colonial authority.

Captain Laxmi's experiences in the INA were transformative. She witnessed firsthand the horrors of war, the sacrifices of her comrades, and the brutal realities of colonial oppression. These experiences deepened her resolve to fight for India's independence and instilled in her a lifelong commitment to justice and equality.

Netaji Subhash Chandra Bose supervising the women soldiers of the INA along with Captain Laxmi Sahgal

Later Years & Struggle in Politics

The defeat of the Axis powers in World War II and the subsequent collapse of the INA marked the end of a crucial chapter in Laxmi Sahgal's life. She was captured by British forces in May 1945 and was held as a prisoner of war. However, her indomitable spirit remained unbroken. Upon her release in 1946, she returned to India, where she continued her medical practice and joined the Communist Party of India (CPI).

Laxmi's entry into politics was driven by her commitment to social justice and her desire to fight for the rights of the marginalized and oppressed. She believed that true freedom could only be achieved when the socio-economic disparities in the country were addressed. Her association with the CPI and later the Communist Party of India (Marxist) saw her actively participating in various movements for workers' rights, women's rights, and social equality.

One of her most notable political endeavours was her involvement in the All India Democratic Women's Association (AIDWA), where she worked tirelessly to uplift the status of women and address issues such as dowry, domestic violence, and gender discrimination. Her work with AIDWA and other grassroots organizations earned her immense respect and admiration across the country.

To comprehend better, the dazzling chronology of Captain Laxmi Sahgal's political and social career could thus be elaborated in the following way: Lakshmi became a member of the Communist Party of India (Marxist) in 1971. She coordinated rescue camps and medical assistance for refugees from Bangladesh who poured into India during the Bangladesh crisis in Calcutta. She spearheaded many of the organization's initiatives and campaigns as one of the original members of the All India Democratic Women's Association in 1981. She fought to bring peace to Kanpur after the anti-Sikh riots of 1984, led a medical team to Bhopal in the wake of the gas catastrophe in December 1984, and was imprisoned in 1996 for her involvement in a campaign against the Miss World pageant in Bangalore. Even at 92 years old, she continued to meet patients daily at her Kanpur clinic in 2006!

Sahgal was nominated as a presidential candidate in the 2002 Indian presidential election by four leftist parties: the Communist Party of India, the Communist Party of India (Marxist), the Revolutionary Socialist Party, and the All India Forward Bloc.

Although she did not win, her candidature was a powerful statement about her enduring legacy and the recognition of her contributions to the nation. Her life's work extended beyond the battlefield, as she continued to inspire generations with her unwavering commitment to justice and equality.

Post-Independence Idea of "Patriotism"

After India's independence in 1947, Laxmi Sahgal's patriotism took on new dimensions. She recognized that the struggle for freedom was far from over; it had merely transitioned from fighting colonial rule to addressing the deep-seated social and economic issues that plagued the newly independent nation. For Laxmi, patriotism meant not only loving one's country but also striving to create a society where every individual had the opportunity to live with dignity and equality.

Laxmi's post-independence patriotism was reflected in her tireless work with marginalized communities. She continued to practice medicine, often providing free healthcare to the poor and underprivileged. Her clinic in Kanpur became a sanctuary for those who could not afford medical treatment, and her compassion and dedication earned her the affectionate title of "Amma" (mother) from her patients.

Her involvement in politics and social activism was driven by a deep-seated belief that true freedom could only be achieved through social and economic justice. She fought against the exploitation of workers, campaigned for women's rights, and championed the cause of the oppressed. Her commitment to these causes was unwavering, and she remained a vocal advocate for justice and equality throughout her life.

Laxmi Sahgal's patriotism was not limited to the boundaries of India. She was deeply concerned about global issues of injustice and inequality. She spoke out against imperialism, colonialism, and the exploitation of developing nations by powerful countries. Her internationalist outlook and solidarity with oppressed peoples worldwide were a testament to her belief in a just and equitable world.

Death and Legacy

Captain Laxmi Sahgal passed away on July 23, 2012, at the age of 97, leaving behind a legacy that continues to inspire and empower. Her life story is a testament to the power of conviction, courage, and compassion. She was a trailblazer who broke barriers and shattered stereotypes, proving that women could be formidable leaders in both war and peace.

Her contributions to the Indian freedom struggle and her relentless efforts to champion the cause of social justice have left an indelible mark on the nation's history. She remains an enduring symbol of the strength and resilience of Indian women, and her story serves as a beacon of hope and inspiration for all those who dare to dream and strive for a better world.

Captain Laxmi Sahgal's legacy is preserved through the countless lives she touched and the movements she inspired. She is remembered not only as a revolutionary leader but also as a compassionate healer and a relentless advocate for justice. Her life's work continues to resonate with those who seek to create a just and equitable society.

As we reflect on the life and legacy of Captain Laxmi Sahgal, we are reminded that the fight for freedom and justice is a continuous journey. Her unwavering spirit and dedication to the cause of the oppressed serve as a powerful reminder that each of us has the potential to make a difference. Captain Laxmi Sahgal's story is not just a chapter in the history of India's struggle for independence; it is a timeless tale of courage, resilience, and the enduring power of the human spirit.

Her life is a call to action, urging us to carry forward her legacy of compassion, justice, and unwavering dedication to the cause of the oppressed. As we honour her memory, let us draw inspiration from her example and strive to create a world where freedom, equality, and justice are not just ideals but lived realities for all. Captain Laxmi Sahgal's story is a beacon of hope, reminding us that the spirit of revolution lives on in each of us...

An 'homage'...

As we conclude this exploration of the lives and sacrifices of India's revolutionaries, it is vital to ponder the true meaning of independence. These brave souls did not fight merely for the physical withdrawal of colonial power but for the reclamation of our nation's soul - its dignity, identity, and the right to self-determination. Yet, as we celebrate the freedom they so dearly won, we must confront an uncomfortable question: Psychologically and from a 'mindset' perspective, are we truly independent?

Even as the tricolour waves proudly across the nation, the shadows of neo-colonialism linger - manifesting in economic dependencies, cultural dominance, and the pervasive influence of foreign ideologies that subtly shape our policies and aspirations. The visible chains of the past may have been broken, but the invisible ones, woven into the fabric of globalisation and modernity, still threaten our sovereignty. The revolutionaries of yore fought against an overt oppressor; today's struggle is against the insidious forces that seek to compromise our autonomy under the guise of progress and development.

To genuinely honour the legacy of these revolutionaries, it is incumbent upon us to cultivate a mindset that is both vigilant and resilient. This means embracing a spirit of self-reliance, fostering innovation rooted in our unique cultural and intellectual heritage, and critically examining the influences that shape our national consciousness. We must actively work to dismantle the remnants of colonial thought that persist in our institutions, education systems, and economic structures, ensuring that our path forward is guided by the principles of justice, equity, and self-respect that our forebears envisioned.

In countering neo-colonialism, we must assert our right to define our destiny - economically, culturally, and politically. This involves strengthening our local economies, protecting our cultural narratives from dilution, and engaging with the world on terms that reflect our values and aspirations. By doing so, we pay true homage to the revolutionaries who gave their lives not just for a free India, but for an India that could stand tall and sovereign globally.

Let their sacrifices be more than just memories; let them be a clarion call for us to continue the struggle for true independence - a struggle that demands not only the liberation of the body but the emancipation of the mind and spirit. In this way, we ensure that the India they dreamed of, an India that is free, proud, and self-determined, becomes a living reality.

My name is Prathamesh Govind Mendki, and for more feedback (or, constructive criticism), you can reach out to me at mendkiprathamesh97@gmail.com

Bibliography

1. *Moffat, Chris. **India's Revolutionary Inheritance**.* Cambridge University Press, 2019. - Focuses on Bhagat Singh and the legacy of Indian revolutionaries.
2. *Chattopadhyay, Gautam. **Revolutionaries of India**.* OUP India, 2020. - Covers a wide range of revolutionaries, including Subhash Chandra Bose, Chandrashekhar Azad, and others.
3. *Mukherjee, Rudrangshu. **The Penguin Gandhi Reader**.* Penguin Books, 2021. - Offers context on the interplay between non-violent and revolutionary approaches, relevant to figures like Madan Lal Dhingra.
4. *Brown, Judith M. **Waiting for Swaraj: The Last Days of Indian Nationalism**.* Cambridge University Press, 2018. - Provides insights into the last phases of revolutionary movements.
5. *Sampath, Vikram. **Savarkar (Part 1 & 2)**.* Penguin Random House India, 2019. - Provides a beautiful insight into the life of Swatantraveer Vinayak Damodar Savarkar
6. *Wadia, R. D. **Lives of the Indian Revolutionaries**.* Macmillan, 2022. - A comprehensive source on revolutionaries like Vasudev Balwant Phadke and Khudiram Bose.
7. *Raj, Nandini. **Freedom Fighters of India: From Phadke to Sehgal**.* Routledge, 2023. - Discusses the trajectory of armed struggle in India's independence.
8. *Gupta, Manmathnath. **History of the Indian Revolutionary Movement**.* Somaiya Publications, 1972. - Analyzes the strategies and impacts of revolutionary actions in British India (The author himself was involved in the 'Kakori' Train Action).
9. *Bose, Sugata. **His Majesty's Opponent: Subhas Chandra Bose and India's Struggle Against Empire**.* Harvard University Press, 2019. - A detailed account of Subhas Chandra Bose's role in India's fight for independence.
10. *Gandhi, Rajmohan. **Rebels Against the Raj**.* HarperCollins, 2021. - Explores the lives of revolutionaries who challenged British rule.
11. *Rao, Anupama. **The Caste Question: Dalits and the Politics of Modern India**.* University of California Press, 2021. - Provides a perspective on how caste intersected with the revolutionary struggle, relevant to figures like Alluri Sitaram Raju.

12. *Majumdar, Sumit.* **Khudiram Bose and the Indian Revolutionary Movement**. Oxford University Press, 2019. - Focuses on Khudiram Bose's role in the revolutionary movement.

13. *Sanyal, Purabi Roy.* **Chandrashekhar Azad: The Hero of Kakori Conspiracy**. Hachette India, 2022. - Offers a detailed biography of Chandrashekhar Azad.

14. *Sehgal, Pritilata Waddedar.* **The Silent Sentinel: The Life and Times of Pritilata Waddedar**. Orient Blackswan, 2020. - Chronicles the life of Pritilata Waddedar and her role in the revolution.

15. *Jain, Madhu.* **Daughters of the Revolution: Shanti Ghosh and Suniti Choudhary**. Zubaan, 2021. - A biographical work on Shanti Ghosh and Suniti Choudhary.

16. *Verghese, Joseph.* **Sardar Udham Singh: The Revenge of Jallianwala Bagh**. Pan Macmillan, 2022. - Details Sardar Udham Singh's life and his act of revenge against Michael O'Dwyer.

17. *Dixit, Neera.* **The Woman Who Fought: Captain Laxmi Sehgal and the INA**. Penguin India, 2020. - Chronicles the life of Captain Laxmi Sehgal.

18. *Sharma, Sunil.* **The Revolutionary-Who-Waits: Madan Lal Dhingra and the Politics of Sacrifice**. Sage Publications, 2023. - Discusses Madan Lal Dhingra's ideological influences.

19. *Dalal, Deepa.* **Surya Sen and the Chittagong Uprising**. Aleph Book Company, 2020. - Focuses on Surya Sen's leadership during the Chittagong Uprising.

20. *Kumar, Ashok.* **Ashfaqullah Khan: The Forgotten Hero**. Bloomsbury India, 2021. - A detailed study on Ashfaqullah Khan's contribution to the Indian independence struggle.

21. *Bhattacharya, Amit.* **Revolutionary Lives: Stories of India's Freedom Struggle**. Speaking Tiger, 2019. - Contains essays on multiple revolutionaries, offering a collective overview.